THE
JOB
CLOSER

THE
JOB
CLOSER

Time-Saving Techniques for Acing **Resumes, Interviews, Negotiations,** and **More**

STEVE DALTON

Author of *The 2-Hour Job Search*

TEN SPEED PRESS
California | New York

IN LOVING MEMORY OF
THOMAS AND DOROTHY DALTON

Library of Congress Cataloging-in-Publication Data
    Names: Dalton, Steve, 1976-author.
    Title: The job closer : time-saving techniques for acing resumes, interviews,
        negotiations, and more / by Steve Dalton.
    Description: First edition. | [Emeryville, California] : Ten Speed Press, an
        imprint of Random House, a division of Penguin Random House LLC, [2020]
    Identifiers: LCCN 2020035543 (print) | LCCN 2020035544 (ebook) |
        ISBN 9781984856968 (trade paperback) | ISBN 9781984856975 (ebook)
    Subjects: LCSH: Job hunting. | Employment interviewing.
    Classification: LCC HF5382.7 .D358 2020 (print) | LCC HF5382.7 (ebook) |
        DDC 650.14—dc23
    LC record available at https://lccn.loc.gov/2020035543
    LC ebookrecord available at https://lccn.loc.gov/2020035544

Trade Paperback ISBN: 978-1-9848-5696-8
eBook ISBN: 978-1-9848-5697-5

Printed in the United States

Acquiring editor: Julie Bennett | Project editor: Kimmy Tejasindhu
Designer: Lauren Rosenberg
Production manager: Dan Myers
Copyeditor: Kristi Hein | Proofreader: Karen Levy | Indexer: Ken DellaPenta
Publicist: Leilani Zee | Marketer: Monica Stanton

The "Handshake" icons on pages 6, 72, and 142 are by b farias,
from TheNounProject.com

2nd Printing

First Edition

CONTENTS

INTRODUCTION

The real voyage of discovery consists, not in seeking new landscapes, but in having new eyes.
—Marcel Proust

Prepare to be taken aback.

My students and career center colleagues at Duke's Fuqua School of Business know to expect this from me by now, but others may find my approaches . . . jarring.

I happen to think that there's a best way to do everything in the job search. Not a general best way, but a *specific* best way—a recipe, in other words—that different people can follow to create similarly tasty results.

This is a surprisingly uncommon perspective in the job search world. For example, think back to the last job search article you read. Did it give you actual instructions to follow? Or did it suggest general tips that you'd have to convert into a plan of action yourself? I see way too much of the latter and basically none of the former. Tips are job search junk food—satisfying in the moment but lacking any real nutrition, repackaging conventional wisdom you've heard before into a slightly different format, making it seem new but adding no real value.

It doesn't have to be this way.

Instructions for your job search are possible and frankly should be the norm. Aren't job search experts in a better position to curate all of their tips into a usable format than overwhelmed job seekers conducting their first, second, or even tenth search?

So, I created such a set of instructions for job search networking in my first book, *The 2-Hour Job Search (2HJS)* and eight years later I'm finally able to share with you my sets of instructions for everything *else* in your job search.

Now, some tasks are difficult even with exact instructions. Take assembling furniture from IKEA, for example. Could you imagine what would happen if IKEA replaced their assembly instructions with assembly *tips*? "Consider attaching the largest pieces to one another first," or "Try to identify pieces that seem to naturally fit together"? There would be a revolt of literally global proportions, or at least a dramatic disruption in the Swedish meatball and lingonberry supply chains.

Rest assured, I am not going to do that to you. Like you, I roll my eyes when I hear old career maxims such as these trotted out:

- "The job search is a full-time job." (If it was, how would people with full-time jobs ever find other jobs?)
- "Sell yourself!" (Few people enjoy selling themselves, and fewer still enjoy hearing others sell *them*selves, so basically everyone hates this.)
- "Put yourself out there!" (If you're charming and extroverted, great advice! If not, terrible advice!)
- "Job searching is an art, not a science." ("I was much better at art than science.")

This book doesn't do tips, and it doesn't do conventional wisdom. It does frameworks—techniques you can immediately use to find the right job faster. A career center that fits in your pocket, if you will.

Now, some of these frameworks may not work for you—some may even anger you—but if you're in a pinch, *any* of these frameworks will be better than no framework at all, and you'll find many of them are much more than just serviceable. They'd better be, as they are approaches I've refined over fifteen years as a career coach and literally thousands of attempts.

To be fair, my goal here isn't to give you perfect solutions; it is to give you the best readily-available solutions. Don't think brain surgery; think the Heimlich maneuver. Simple techniques that you don't have to be a rocket scientist to grasp and that can be implemented on short notice even during incredibly stressful circumstances.

In *2HJS*, I purposely focused on the one part of the job search every other job search book *insisted* was an art rather than a science: networking for interviews. Amazingly, job seekers of all networking proficiencies found my specificity helpful, and I started getting requests for what frameworks I could offer for the *other* parts of the job search, from preparing a resume to interviewing well. I had thoughts on those, but no frameworks yet, so people asked me for book recommendations.

I was stumped. I didn't *like* any books on those topics—especially back in 2012 when *2HJS* first came out. Most books seemed to complicate every element of the job search rather than simplify. You don't really need a book on the top one hundred interview questions you need to master. As you'll soon learn, you really just need to know how to answer the first several well, and the rest is gravy.

So I decided to again build my own frameworks, this time for answering interview questions, writing cover letters, and everything else, primarily as a way to get my students and *2HJS* readers back to *networking* as quickly as possible due to its far greater importance. Students and readers alike seemed to know this was true, yet still the item they fretted over most was their resume, the least important element of their job search portfolio.

(Did that last bit about the relative unimportance of resumes surprise you? If so, brace yourself. Resumes may still be necessary, but they have lost their crown jewel status.)

Something had to give. The job search has gotten *way* more complex in the last thirty years, but job seekers didn't suddenly get more time! That means that the same amount of time that used to *just* go toward resumes, cover letters, and interview prep must now include LinkedIn, online job search engines, resume keyword optimization, social media, and other prep as well. Further complicating matters, each of those items has a different *level* of importance, so the solution is not merely spending an equal amount of time on each. Modern job seekers must figure out how to allocate their limited time and energy across all the various job search skills according to each one's relative importance.

Most job seekers don't know how to do this however; they've never been taught. Even worse, most career coaches haven't been taught the importance of prioritization either. The net result is that we get inundated by articles and books that present every single mundane element of the job search as if it were a matter of life or death. However, when you focus on everything, you focus on nothing.

Neither you nor I have time for that. Like my students, you probably want to know how *little* time you can spend on everything for it to be "good enough" rather than spending years trying to get it all to be perfect before embarking. That's where I come in.

Just as the Heimlich maneuver provides a quick, good-enough solution to someone who's choking, this book provides you with quick, good-enough solutions for every element of the job search (minus networking, which I already address in *2HJS*). In other words, the goal of this book is not to help you create perfect resumes, cover letters, or anything else—because no such things exist.

Nobody agrees on what a 100-percent-perfect resume or cover letter looks like. It breaks my heart when job seekers tell me about spending hundreds of dollars on a professional resume writer to get their resume *just right*, only to have a different resume writer tell them their resume is all wrong and that they need to start over and spend hundreds of dollars more to get it right for real this time. That's the nightmare of the modern job search. You will encounter a lot of conflicting advice; your challenge is to determine which information you find most credible.

So why should you believe this particular book is credible? Because, like I said, I don't do tips—vague advice like "get organized" or "stay positive." I do instructions. Exclusively. That means that you can follow my recipe exactly and bake a cake that looks and tastes just the way it does when *I* follow the recipe.

This approach opens itself to a lot of critique, and that is the point. It's hard to disagree with lists of tips, because there's nothing to test. Instructions, however, can be tested. This also means they can be improved: made simpler, faster, more effective, and so on.

So prepare to be taken aback.

What I present to you in this book are recipes for all common scenarios that job seekers must be prepared to handle. If you follow them precisely, I can assure you that your job search cake will rise.

These frameworks are indeed more like baking than cooking. In cooking, mistakes can be made and corrected at the end of the cooking process by adjusting ingredients and seasonings to make the final product palatable; in baking, however, if you fail to add an ingredient, or fail to add it at the right time or in the right amount, your cake won't rise and there's no saving it later.

In this book, I will point out when a step is more like *baking* (where precision is critical) than *cooking* (where approximation is OK), so that you know when you can experiment without risk. However, if you don't like the idea of experimenting *at all* and you just want to follow instructions exactly—treating your job search just as you'd treat the step-by-step construction of an IKEA bookshelf—you will achieve more than basic proficiency quickly and without wasted effort. Furthermore, thanks to the rubrics at the end of each chapter, you will always know *when* you have achieved good-enough performance as well, freeing you to begin the next step of your search.

A word of caution: For many, this process will require forgetting things you thought you knew about job searching in order to learn new, more effective approaches. That's why I want to tell you about IDEO's Project Mood Chart before we finish this introduction.

The Mood Chart plots the mood of teams (y-axis) over the duration (x-axis) of a challenging project. The chart follows a basic "U"-shaped curve, with peaks at both ends and a valley in the middle (you can find it online if you would like a visual aid). At first, teams start off in a positive mood (a peak labeled "Hope"), then after dipping down into a valley where the mood becomes decidedly negative, teams address the problems they encountered in order to emerge on the other side of the project, happy again and smarter for the effort (a second peak beyond the valley that is labeled "Confidence").

What I love most about the IDEO Project Mood Chart is what they label the valley where the team's mood turns negative—Insight. Learning isn't always fun, but it is the precursor to proficiency. You will get there if you adopt the frameworks I show you, and your confidence will soar as a result.

At Fuqua, we show this chart to all new students to prepare them for the challenges ahead, job search–related and otherwise. Furthermore, we tell them that we will *actively* push them down into the Valley of Insight so that they can emerge on the other side as stronger job seekers as quickly as possible.

This book similarly will push you into the Valley of Insight. My frameworks may seem foreign and counterintuitive at first, but by learning and adopting them, with every hour of practice you put in you will steadily improve your odds of employment and advancement.

So prepare to be taken aback!

PART 1

Before the Interview

CHAPTER 1

Choosing a Career

What should I do with my life?

Ah, the million-dollar question.

So, I have bad news and good news. The bad news is that in over a decade of doing this work, I have yet to find a comprehensive test, diagnostic, or fun personality quiz that answers this question effectively. I think it's because it's impossible. We are all simply too different.

The good news is that there are a number of efficient techniques that I think *help* answer this question in a tangible, actionable way—one that doesn't involve dozens of hours of self-analysis and journaling. In this chapter, I'll walk you through these techniques.

Wait, what's wrong with spending dozens of hours self-analyzing and journaling?

Oh, pardon me. In the proper context, these can be delightful activities. However, stakes have risen recently, particularly for people who provide for others or have incurred debt. (So, basically everyone.) Let's look at college students as an example of these rising stakes.

Between 1989 and 2016, tuition grew eight times faster than inflation-adjusted wages[1,2,3] and the purchasing power of our wages today is actually lower than it was in the early 1970s.[4] Furthermore, a few decades ago, higher education was a golden ticket to a better life. An undergraduate degree (regardless of major) used to be a standalone asset in your job search, but now many of those same jobs require graduate degrees, meaning even more years of expensive tuition.

Similarly, spending a dozen or so hours on self-analysis to identify your preferred work environments, locations, or responsibilities might have been a justifiable exercise a few years ago. However, today we are in the age of monopsony (think "buyer's market"), in which larger employers can control the type, number, and pay of jobs they make available. These larger employers have done all they can to replace high-paying jobs with low-paying ones and eliminate others to save on costs, resulting in employees working longer before retiring and mid-career employees staying in their "entry level" jobs longer because there are fewer and fewer positions left to be promoted into. Nobody is safe.

So, rather than starting from ideal conditions and working backward, I'd rather work forward from the worst-case scenario (undesired unemployment) as a starting point to try to find a career that captures as many bright spots as possible in the shortest amount of time. We can focus on the things we want to be *sure* we'll enjoy attaining from our next job; then we'll refine our goals as we go along to factor in any complications we encounter or insights we learn along the way.

In the end, the best way to identify and evaluate potential careers is to talk to people who currently have them to see if what they like about their work resonates with you. Not only does this approach help you identify sectors where you establish rapport and trust quicker than in others (an indication that you're headed in the right direction), but it also humanizes you in the process. Ultimately, employers don't hire people; *people* hire people. Thus, you need to get to know them and vice versa.

Does that mean I have to network?

Absolutely.

How can I network if I don't know what I want to do yet?

Honestly, that makes networking easier, because you will be most interested in genuinely learning rather than selling yourself or trying to parlay the conversation into a job interview.

What if I don't like networking?

I don't like flu shots, but I get them every year because they help me avoid becoming sick.

Interestingly, though, I hate flu shots now a lot less than I used to, just from having gotten them so many times before. You'll find the same happens with your perception of networking.

Furthermore, networking just works. For every job that goes to an online applicant, twelve jobs go to internal referrals.[5] Networking is the only way to systematically get referrals, so transitively it is the only systematic way to get interviews.

You'll find that networking for information is a great way to become comfortable networking for jobs. I once worked with a job seeker trying to leave fundraising who shared this wonderful fundraising truism: "When you ask for money, you get time; when you ask for time, you get money." The job search is the same way. When you seek information, you get job leads, and when you seek job leads, you get information (and not always the helpful kind). Let your genuine curiosity be your guide.

Our goal before we start developing these referrals is to narrow our scope to just three candidate careers, so that is what we are aiming for in this chapter.

Why only three candidate careers?

Because when you can narrow your scope down to three candidate careers, you are able to create a LAMP list.

What's a LAMP list?

The LAMP list (List-Alumni-Motivation-Posting) is the foundational concept of my first book. It's essentially a strategy guide that tells you which target employers are most worth your finite amount of energy, time, and pain tolerance for job searching—all within just seventy minutes of effort. This may seem far-fetched, but you accomplish this by swapping perfection for speed, identifying forty target employers and three pieces of data for each that are easy to find and predictive of success.

For the purpose of selecting a career path, you can use a LAMP list to identify five employers (and an ordered list of backups) to begin targeting those three possible career paths in a systematic, iterative fashion, learning enough about each as you go to determine if you favor one or two paths over the other(s), in which case you'd simply remake your LAMP list rather than try to update your existing one.

By focusing on no more than three career paths (spread across five different target employers) at one time, you ensure you don't spread yourself too thin. You will learn as you go—what you learn from one video game company will help you establish credibility with another, and so on.

What if I can't even come up with three career paths?

That's what we'll work on for the remainder of this chapter: how to quickly identify target career paths of interest so that you can start investigating them immediately.

Sadly, there is no magic bullet or single survey you can take that will provide answers to all, so I'm going to introduce you to a number of different techniques that don't take very long but can get you pointed in the right direction quickly and at minimal (or no) cost.

What are the techniques?

I like how you think! Why waste time? Here they are, listed roughly in chronological order:

#	TECHNIQUE	TIME (APPROXIMATE)
1	"You Bet Your Life" exercise	1 min
2	"Brain Dump" exercise	2 min
3	StrengthsFinder + "How Your Talents Add Value" exercise	60 min each
4	Informational meetings	30 min each
5	Mindful reading	ongoing

In the remainder of this chapter I will take you through each one.

TECHNIQUE #1: "YOU BET YOUR LIFE" EXERCISE (1 min)

Open the stopwatch on your phone. For real; just do it now.

You will have only one minute to answer this question, and your life depends on answering it correctly. Furthermore, you get only one guess. Ready? Here's the question:

Name a single professional skill or ability in which you are most confident you are in the top 1 percent of the world. Your minute starts now.

Don't worry. I'll wait.

Got it? Good!

Sorry to do that whole "making you bet your life" thing, but I find that this exercise—both the time pressure and the focus on one superlative skill rather than a laundry list of good skills—tends to be clarifying for many of the job seekers with whom I work.

If nothing else, make sure that any job you accept in the future takes advantage of this one skill. I mean, you just bet your life on it; why not try to find a way to get paid for it? Again, my approach for career selection is both iterative—meaning we'll investigate a few different options partway before committing to a path—and bottom-up—meaning we'll start from nothing and identify the cornerstones of our future career rather than starting from an ideal job and picking what concessions to make first (a frustrating and inherently negative exercise). Consider this skill or ability the first cornerstone of your future career.

In some way, this one skill should be compensated in what you do next. If you are struggling to find firms willing to pay for your elite Tetris-playing ability, however, you may want to reinterpret your skill more figuratively than literally. For example, in what way is your Tetris ability exceptional? Is it your pattern recognition? Your spatial creativity? Your balance of short-term and long-term planning? Consider your answer more broadly if you are struggling to connect your "Bet Your Life" response to a profession right away.

KEY BENEFIT: Cutting through the noise. If your ability to provide for yourself and your loved ones depends on one thing, this should be it.

TECHNIQUE #2: "BRAIN DUMP" EXERCISE (2 min)

This exercise is similarly focused on speed. Starting right now, write down every job that you think you would enjoy doing and could feasibly be or become qualified for one day (so while becoming the next Michael Jordan is not in the cards for me, perhaps *coaching* basketball at a junior level could be if I was willing to pay my dues).

Keep going until you literally can't think of any more—this generally takes a couple of minutes. However, you have to promise to write every-thing down that meets this description. Every single thing. This general tactic is known as a "brain dump," in which you dump everything out of your head and onto a sheet of paper or spreadsheet.

Many of my job seekers who find themselves stuck in the career selection phase tend to endlessly cycle through all of the options they have in their head, wearing themselves out with self-debate but never actually making any progress. This technique will at least help you avoid that endless churning in your mind.

Then set the list aside for the moment. You may choose to add to it over the next day or two, if you have additional ideas.

This act alone helps you get outside of your own head for a bit. Eventually you will run out of new ideas, which will make it easier to focus on one or more of your favorites from the list you created for further investigation, first through research or informational meetings (we'll talk more about informational meetings later in this chapter during Technique #4).

KEY BENEFIT: Getting out of your own head. Turning a seemingly infinite number of options into a finite list of possibilities.

TECHNIQUE #3: STRENGTHSFINDER + "HOW YOUR TALENTS ADD VALUE" EXERCISE (60 min each)

Whenever I would take a report card home, my parents' attention would always go to the lowest grade. (FYI, it was penmanship. My dreams of being 2nd grade valedictorian were dashed by a subject that no longer exists.) It's neither good nor bad; it's just human nature to focus on improving that which we feel needs improvement.

Recently, though, there's been a revolution in the education world called *positive psychology*, that states we have more growth potential in enhancing our natural abilities than we do in shoring up our weaknesses. It's a much more pleasant way to live. My favorite resource in the positive psychology space is the StrengthsFinder quiz.

By taking this 177-question quiz compiled by Gallup and available either online or in book form (sadly, it does require a nominal fee to take the quiz), you will learn which five of thirty-four talent themes you most strongly possess. (The theory is that your innate talents plus focused effort become your strengths.)

While it may sound like any other personality test that you can get from the internet, this one is based on a large data set (fifteen million people have taken it to date), and I find that it actually does a good job of giving you words for what makes you special and uniquely talented. The odds that you would have the same Top 5 talent themes as another person are one in 275,000. The odds that you have the same Top 5 in the same *order* are one in 33.4 million.

Indeed, the order of your Top 5 also matters. Mine are (1) Strategic, (2) Learner, (3) Activator, (4) Command, (5) Analytical. Think of this ranking as your own personal computer code—the troubleshooting script you unconsciously run through when making decisions. I, for example, almost always start by identifying several different paths forward (a hallmark of those with the Strategic talent theme) to open my mind up to nonobvious solutions. Occasionally, it means I overthink relatively simple decisions, like how to arrange my dishes in the dishwasher, but generally it's a skill that has served me well and one my colleagues seem to value.

Furthermore, your Top 5 talent themes interact with one another, rather than presenting themselves the same way in anyone who possesses them. My Strategic talent, for example, is heavily influenced by my Learner and Activator, and all are very much at the heart of *2HJS* and this book. For example, from what sources can I draw inspiration (Learner) to quickly give others a good-enough, Heimlich maneuver–like solution (Strategic) to immediately move from idea to action (Activator) in their job search? (My Command, incidentally, is what makes me want to codify these approaches in books to get others to try them out for themselves.)

Just this year, we introduced an exercise for our Duke MBAs called "How Your Talents Add Value" to help drive this point home for them. We presented them with four "buckets" of work: (1) Making things happen, (2) Collaborating with others, (3) Leading and influencing others, and (4) Solving challenging problems. We then asked our students to pick *two* of their Top 5 talent themes that they must regularly combine in order to accomplish each bucket of work. They were instructed to put in their own words how they used these talent themes in tandem to do good work and then to describe an example where they did so.

At heart, everyone must be able to complete all four of those buckets of work, but *how* we go about accomplishing them is completely unique. Furthermore, if someone else were to attempt your approach (or you theirs), it simply wouldn't work. We've all refined our personal styles over many years—decades, even—and we've learned to make them work.

However, most of us don't realize we *have* styles, and fewer still have the ability to *describe* them to a potential employer. That's why the How Your Talents Add Value exercise is so powerful as a follow-on to StrengthsFinder. It gives you the confidence to quickly answer "yes" when asked if you know how your talents add value to organizations. That confidence benefits you even when that question is never explicitly asked. These answers take days, weeks, or months to discover and develop, however, so better to start that exploration sooner rather than later.

I feel such affection for the StrengthsFinder test and the How Your Talents Add Value exercise because learning your top talent themes not only helps you focus on what makes you excellent rather than mediocre, but it also gives you ownable language that is more insightful than job seeker clichés like "I'm a good problem solver" or "I'm solutions-focused." *How* are you a good problem solver, exactly? *How* do you identify solutions? Knowing those answers about your signature style makes resumes easier to draft, cover letters easier to write, interview questions easier to answer, and beyond.

Neither StrengthsFinder nor the How Your Talents Add Value exercise will tell you what job you should pursue, but they will give you suggestions for work situations in which you will naturally and intuitively thrive, making it easier for you to evaluate potential career paths for both sustainability and personal fulfillment.

If you find this approach enlightening, I recommend purchasing the full ordered list of your thirty-four talent themes from Gallup. The value in doing this is that you will receive a detailed report on your Top 10 (considered more stable over time than your Top 5, which tend to fluctuate) while also allowing you to view your *least* developed talent themes. StrengthsFinder theory states that, while you could work very hard to slightly improve those bottom talent themes, that time would be better spent further enhancing your top ones and identifying teammates innately gifted in your weaker themes who can help you when the need arises.

My thirty-fourth and last talent theme is Harmony. Knowing this helps me to understand that if I'm faced with a situation where I need to ensure that everyone is getting along, it's better for me to reach out to a colleague who is better able to (and who may even enjoy!) mediating and raising team morale. They, in turn, will appreciate being given an opportunity to shine at something they intuitively do well. It's the classic make-or-buy decision. (Plus, the first time you pull this feat off, you'll feel like you pulled off a bank heist! Except nobody lost any money, and you don't risk prison and all that. It's an analogy.)

You may wish to know which talent themes align best with which careers, but the answer to that is "whichever ones you have." Everything still more or less boils down to those four buckets of work mentioned earlier; it's less about what your Top 5 are and more about whether you know and can explain how you'll adapt them to the working circumstances of a particular role. Some translations will be easier than others, yes, but with this information you can make a better call about whether making a certain profession work is worth the effort.

TECHNIQUE #4: INFORMATIONAL MEETINGS (30 min each)

Informational meetings (informationals, for short) are a form of information gathering in which you control the agenda, rather than the more traditional form of interviewing, in which the employer manages the agenda. Informationals allow job seekers a chance to learn about potential careers and employers by asking current employees why they enjoy doing what they do where they do it, ideally in a systematic and purposeful fashion.

I discuss informationals at length in *2HJS*, so if you'd like more information about how best to do those, please read that book's sections on the TIARA (Trends-Insights-Advice-Resources-Assignments) Framework. TIARA provides you with a road map for turning strangers into advocates within a single thirty-minute informational by using a series of fun and flattering-to-answer questions to first cast them as experts in their field before shifting the focus of your questions to cast them as potential mentors.

Essentially, TIARA gives you a script for subtly asking strangers: "Why *are* you so good at your job?" a few different ways so that they enjoy talking to you (since talking to you means getting to talk positively about themselves) and are willing to advocate for you to their peers. However, you will also genuinely learn a lot about the role, organization, and sector in the process.

Informational meetings effectively serve double duty. Each one makes you smarter about the space you're seeking to enter while—more importantly—giving you one more set of eyes and ears (in the form of your new advocate) watching out for job opportunities on your behalf, steadily increasing your odds of interviews and offers over time as you have more and more conversations.

I particularly like informationals if you are in a situation where your list of top-tier potential career paths is greater than three—too many to create a LAMP list, but enough that one informational apiece (at thirty minutes each) seems like a feasible endeavor. One data point for each may not seem like a lot, but you'd be surprised how quickly a single conversation can invigorate—or destroy—your interest in a particular career path!

TECHNIQUE #5: READING MINDFULLY (ongoing)

Our final approach for career selection consists only of that which you already do: surfing the internet.

Simply do the normal business/industry-related reading you do in your spare time (books and magazines are also eligible for consideration). However, *now* I want you to start a habit of reading mindfully, so that whenever you read about an organization doing interesting work, you make a note of that organization's name and sector, since it is a potential employer.

Every day we acquire so much knowledge *for free*; I want to find a way to get you paid for it. Whatever you get smarter at and continue to learn about without even trying (or getting compensated for) is an avenue you should at least consider as a potential career path.

Once this habit is established, you'll start to spot some patterns. It may not necessarily reveal the name of your profession-to-be, but it will help you clarify your genuine interests. Whenever possible, I find it is best not to fight gravity, since gravity always wins.

So which technique works best?

Don't think of these techniques as working in isolation; much as we did with StrengthsFinder test results and the How Your Talents Add Value exercise, think of them as working in tandem.

Each one provides a meaningful data point, but considered together they start to tell a story that helps you expand your consideration set and escape the box you or your environment may have wittingly or unwittingly created for you. Even the act of turning all of the ideas in your head into a written list will start converting the churning anxiety cycle in your brain into something much more finite and actionable.

That said, if you've tried all the above techniques and are still looking for further exploration opportunities, allow me to heartily recommend the Odyssey Planning exercise from *Designing Your Life*, an excellent book by Stanford professors Dave Evans and Bill Burnett.

The core message of their book is that there is no such thing as a "best possible life." Instead, there are many possible lives—you just need to decide which one to pursue first. What I find so appealing about *Designing Your Life* is how it provides practical exercises for those seeking to identify fulfillment, both personally and professionally. To that end, the Odyssey Planning exercise consists of first creating a plausible five-year plan for yourself and rating that plan based on four metrics: enjoyment, resources, confidence, and personal coherence. Then, the process is followed by . . . a twist so delicious I wouldn't dare spoil it here. My students at Duke have loved this exercise for years now, and I think you would enjoy it too.

And finally, recognize that we don't need to solve all of this today. We'll identify the path ahead one step at a time. Just hang in there and stay curious about the future.

CHAPTER CHECKLIST

Do you have one or more career paths you want to investigate first?

TROUBLESHOOTING

What if I have a lot of debt and/or other obligations and need to take a particular job I'm not excited about to satisfy those demands?

Ultimately, only you know your liquidity and your risk tolerance. However, I see too many job seekers avoid making good-faith attempts to get the job they *really* want because pursuing a "safe" career—for example, one they've done before or one where there is great need—is so much easier than making a *desired* change.

That's not to say you should ignore your debt or obligations! I simply point this out to highlight that there is no longer any such thing as a "safe" career. It may be "safe" for a year or two, but you can still get laid off, especially once the employer identifies that you don't have your heart in your work. Furthermore, job seekers tend to underestimate how very costly switching away from a dispiriting job can be, both in terms of money lost while between jobs and stress for themselves and their loved ones. You can ignore your heart for a while, but not indefinitely. It will come for you eventually, so better to make peace with it sooner than later.

I recommend creating an honest budget. By "honest" I mean one anchored in the reality of providing for your loved ones and paying off your debts rather than on what the average salaries are for someone in your profession with your level of experience.

I took a big pay cut to leave marketing for a career coaching role back in 2005, but the ability to earn a living addressing a universal source of anxiety—the ability to secure employment—was well worth every dollar I gave up in salary. I no longer hated waking up in the morning and heading to the office! Quite the opposite, in fact. And my Sundays were no longer spent dreading the Monday to follow.

The cost? I paid off my student loans more slowly than I would have had I stayed in marketing. Granted, this was more than a decade ago, when student debt burdens were lower relative to salary than they are today, but to me this makes finding a career you don't dread even more critical, as missed paychecks due to layoffs—which tend to disproportionately (though not exclusively) impact those who dislike their work— can quickly negate any short-term salary advantage that a more lucrative but demotivating career provides.

Furthermore, those who genuinely enjoy their work tend to expand their roles and worth to their organizations over time, so while a less lucrative career may mean less money in the short term, the enhanced growth prospects may make it a better long-term bet than stagnating in a job you dislike, with the added bonus of enjoying those eight to twelve hours a day instead of enduring them.

Just remember that employers don't really care how much you need a job when deciding whom to lay off. The only way to shield yourself from unplanned unemployment is excellence at what you do, and excellence seems to be accessible only to those who find their work engaging. Thus, account for your immediate needs, yes, but recognize that *depletion* is not sustainable. If you feel yourself getting weaker each day, make a change as soon as possible.

What if my dream job is totally unrelated to what I'm doing now?

How fast can you learn?

A former marketing colleague of mine left the field around the same time I did to eventually pursue a career in voice acting. She had never acted professionally before, but she always

continued

enjoyed practicing accents and performing in a variety of settings. Her friends and classmates thought she had lost her mind, but she suddenly cared about her work, *wanting* to get better every day.

It was difficult in the short term, mostly because of the voices in her own head (ugh) rather than those of others, but eventually she landed her first gig. And a second. And a third. And now she's a successful entrepreneur and a featured performer in a major video game franchise, despite not entering the industry until her thirties.

Seniority used to be a source of security in the workplace, but now employers are looking at senior employees as layoff targets even more aggressively, since they represent greater savings than less-experienced ones. Again, excellence at your craft is the only way to ensure that you hold on to your job, and even that is never foolproof. However, it does make finding a new role much easier than if you never liked that job you just left in the first place.

My recommendation: dip your foot in the pool before you dive in. Can you take a class or shadow someone to get a better sense for what a potential major career change may look like? Create a detailed budget to identify whether your likely salary could pay off your financial obligations (which is *distinctly* different from finding a salary that matches your current one—too frequently I see job seekers unwilling to consider any pay cuts to leave a job they dislike, regardless of their actual financial *needs*, effectively locking themselves in a prison of their own making).

In marketing, I worked *really* hard to be mediocre, while the people at the desks next to me seemed to excel without even trying. It was a dehumanizing way to live, and I wouldn't wish it on anyone. In retrospect, I'm glad I had such a close-up view of my competition for retention and advancement. I'd never be able to keep up with them, and today I see that I didn't want to in the first place.

Discretion is indeed the better part of valor, but that perspective is hard to embrace when you haven't yet identified any alternatives.

What if I have family or loved ones who would possibly be negatively impacted by any career choice or change I make?

Short answer: bring them into the decision. Explain your rationale. You may not be able to get their full buy-in immediately, but it starts a conversation that may result in a win-win. For example, perhaps you can agree on a time or budget limit for you to explore your alternative career without reservation before returning to your current one or opting for another.

There comes a time when we all must advocate for what we want from our brief time on this planet. It's OK to start that process before you have an exact picture of what exactly you want. Answers to these literally life-defining questions usually take time and trial and error, so the more hands you're able to summon on deck to help make this decision, the better.

Furthermore, our loved ones and support network often know when we want something different before we do. The exercises outlined in this chapter give you a way to turn this subtext into real conversation and benefit from your loved ones' perspectives as well.

Perhaps a career transition is *not* feasible right now, but you'll be surprised at how often your support network can and will step up with ideas, support, and resources once they know what it is that you truly want.

What if "normal" careers don't really appeal to me?

I think every "normal" job has been optimized to within an inch of its life, but where's the fun in that?

The real opportunity (and the most interesting work, I'd argue) for anyone who would ask this question is at the margins

continued

of normalcy: either combining one or more sectors or roles that others haven't thought to combine, or applying existing skills in a new venue, or starting your own venture to do the work that may not pay well immediately but will inspire you to wake up every morning and keep making your business better until it *does* pay the bills.

If mainstream careers seem unsatisfying, then welcome to the club! It was *obsession* that led me to career services, not a healthy interest in helping others. It baffled me—why wasn't *everyone* fixated on this high-stakes struggle that literally every person faces many times in their lives?

So you're not alone, and I think I have a visualization that may help.

Envision the "universe of employees" (or significant others, or any other topic, for that matter, where you feel out of the norm) as an old-school, thoroughly used archery target—the kind with a bull's-eye and concentric rings that are worth fewer and fewer points the farther they are from the center.

Naturally, many holes from previous arrows will be clustered around the center, since that is where everyone has been aiming. If you have generally likable and appealing qualities, I would call you a "bull's-eye person"—instantly accessible and largely fungible, meaning there are a lot of other people out there like you who could play a similar role in an organization.

Back to our archery target: as you look at the first ring outside the bull's-eye, then the second, and then the third, you'll see that the farther away from the center you get, the less densely packed and numerous the holes from previous arrows become. If you have traits or interests that are outside the mainstream, I would call you an "outer-ring person." The more unusual you are, the farther from the bull's-eye the ring you occupy. (I consider myself a proud fourth-ring resident.)

Outer-ring people tend to fit best in outer-ring careers—ones where the desired skill set isn't interchangeable with many other careers and to which fewer people may be drawn.

Some of your more mainstream friends, hearing this analogy, might just say, "Well, go find an outer-ring career!" The problem is that, just like outer-ring people, outer-ring careers are fewer and farther between. Also, just because you and a career share the same ring doesn't mean you are compatible.

For example, let's say I discovered a career that's *also* in the fourth ring where I hang out. That career could be clear over on the opposite side of the target from me! In that case, I'd be much closer to literally *any* bull's-eye career than to the majority of fourth-ring careers!

My advice? Don't despair, but don't be soft either. You didn't choose this life, but your search for that proper fit will take longer than your bull's-eye-proximal peers. Furthermore, your path may involve taking some bull's-eye jobs until you're able to find your true match. Just keep an open mind and be sure to pay attention to the careers others ignore, especially those that your self-identified peer group gravitate toward. If you know peers who seem to have found their calling, don't be shy about asking them how they figured it out and when they knew it was right.

Unfortunately, I can't guarantee that you'll ever find your perfect match so it's critical that you enjoy the process of searching as much as possible along the way. Whereas bull's-eye people can get away with postponing happiness and living for tomorrow due to the high likelihood they'll find their match eventually—be it a career match, a relationship match, or a best friend match—it's even *more* important for outer-ring people to live for right now.

And know that you're not alone; you're just an outer-ring person. ☺

CHAPTER 2

Resumes

Aren't there *entire books* devoted to how to write a perfect resume? What makes you think you can tell me how to do it in twenty-three pages?

It starts with acknowledging that *there is no such thing as a perfect resume.*

Intuitively, you may already have known this. As I mentioned in this book's intro, I've talked to a number of job seekers who have spent hours working with career centers or professional resume writers to get their resume "perfect," only to have that dream crumble as soon as they showed it to somebody else with an opinion on resumes. It's devastating. Ask ten different certified resume reviewers, get ten different opinions.

People will confidently tell you that having a perfect CV (resumes and CVs are different documents, but the approach for both is similar, so I will use these terms interchangeably in this chapter) is critical, but *nobody actually agrees on what a perfect resume looks like.* Given this lack of agreement, it seems to me a form of malpractice to tell job seekers to strive for a perfect resume.

However, even if it *were* possible to create a perfect CV with dozens of hours of work, it wouldn't be worth the effort.

How can you say that?!

Hiring managers just don't spend that much time reading resumes.

Seriously?

Indeed. There's even data that backs this up.

A few years ago, TheLadders.com did a study in which they hooked up hiring managers to eye-tracking software and asked them to review a stack of resumes. They found that on average hiring managers spent six seconds per resume.[1]

There are many studies that find variations on the notion that hiring managers don't spend much time reading resumes, but TheLadders' study went a step further. It found *what* exactly hiring managers were looking at during that six seconds. Specifically, they found that 80 percent of hiring managers' attention during that time period was focused on the following information.

- Candidate name
- Employer name(s)
- Job title(s)
- Dates of employment
- Schools attended

Can you spot what they have in common? If not, let me help. Hiring managers spent 4.8 out of those six seconds looking at things *you can't change!*

But that's not the stuff that job seekers agonize over. The agony is over the stuff they *can* change—namely, their bullets. By bullets, I mean the short, bullet-pointed accomplishments one typically lists below each position and over which job seekers have much more control in terms of wording and presentation. However, when you realize that all of those bullet points combined get about 1.2 seconds of attention, spending endless hours on them no longer makes much sense. Even the fastest speed readers wouldn't get through more than a few of them, so it's safe to say most aren't getting read at all.

But if they only spend 1.2 seconds on my bullets, don't any bullets they *do* read have to be perfect?

That's one way to look at it, but it doesn't match the reality of what hiring managers are looking for when screening CVs. Hiring managers are looking for *easy-to-defend candidates*, not perfectly worded bullets—at least in their initial passes through a stack of resumes.

What are easy-to-defend candidates?

They are candidates who could never embarrass a hiring manager, no matter how poorly they interview, due to their pedigree or previous experience.

No hiring manager will ever be criticized if they, for example, bring in a candidate who has done this job before but somewhere else, or one who attended an elite school. However, they could suffer personal embarrassment from bringing in someone unconventional who leaves a negative impression.

In other words, candidates have a hierarchy. Candidates who have done the job before somewhere else will always be considered. Almost as frequently considered are ones who worked for elite employers or attended elite schools (either regionally or more broadly). These pieces of information do not require finessing in our resume, however, and thus don't stress out job seekers—they simply are what they are.

Easy-to-defend candidates are the only ones who are "found" through online job postings, and even then, there's no guarantee. Again, no hiring manager wants to suffer the embarrassment of bringing in a novelty candidate who doesn't match the easy-to-defend descriptions, only to have them perform terribly in the interview. In that case, the hiring manager alone will suffer the black eye. (Note that entry-level candidates are generally easier to defend than mid-career ones, since their credentialing is simpler to assess, they are cheaper to employ, and they represent lower risk if the collaboration fizzles. This explains why the success rate of applying to online job postings tends to decrease as one's experience and wage expectations increase. So, by all means, if you are just starting your career, give online job postings a try to see what your response rate is like from your targeted employers before deciding how to allocate your finite time and energy between applying and networking.)

But what if I'm not an easy-to-defend candidate?

Then your CV is unlikely to be pulled out of a stack of CVs to be read at all. I know the following will sound odd, but this reality should come as a bit of a relief!

Relief?!

Relief from worrying about perfectly wording your bullet points! If you're neither an easy-to-defend candidate nor endorsed by an internal referral, your bullet points are unlikely to get read through any online job posting application (and if you *are* one of those two types of candidates, hiring managers will be predisposed to like anything they read. So even just an error-free resume should suffice to get you an interview).

So why should I even bother?

Great question! Resumes are a necessary evil in the modern job search. You want to try to hit the Goldilocks zone as quickly and efficiently as possible, meaning your resume is neither too cold (underprepared, causing an unprofessional first impression) nor too hot (overprepared, but at the cost of higher-value activities).

That is the goal of this chapter in this book: to help you invest in your resume *enough*, but not too much. Overinvestment is a bottomless pit of cost, energy, and stress that returns little benefit.

So how will I even know when my resume is "done," then?

Another great question! In short, your resume is "done" when it is *objectively* perfect and subjectively good enough.

In English, please.

Objective means something is right or wrong, black or white, true or false; subjective means something is a matter of opinion. Thus, objectively perfect means there is 100-percent consensus among readers that something is correct.

For example, all readers agree that "manager" is correct and "manger" is incorrect when trying to spell the word for one who oversees a particular task or group. Thus, it is an objective matter rather than a subjective one.

On any matter where everyone agrees, that information should absolutely be perfect. For resumes, this typically includes the following items:

- Proper spelling
- Correct grammar
- Aligned margins
- Internally consistent formatting (for example, when mentioning a range of years, don't use 2022-23 in one place and 2022–2023 in another)
- Single font used throughout

Perfection on these items does not definitively prove you have good attention to detail—a universally desirable and *easily judged* skill—but *im*perfection on these items definitively proves you lack it when it really counts.

Furthermore, featuring an objective error in your resume makes it very hard for a potential internal advocate to push for you, since they would not want to be ridiculed as the person who advocated for Manger Guy.

For the purpose of this chapter, we will consider this 100-percent error-free resume our *minimum viable product* (MVP), which we will call Basic Resume for the rest of this chapter.

If a Basic Resume is an MVP, are you telling me that it is good enough for job searching?

I wouldn't go *that* far.

The Basic Resume is simply our baseline—our worst-case scenario, if you will. It is the worst resume we will ever present to the world from this point forward; it is also the last time anyone will agree on your resume.

Everyone will have suggestions for improvement, but they will be just that: suggestions. There will no longer be any objective corrections to make, everything from this point forward will be a matter of subjective opinion (including the remainder of this chapter).

That said, you didn't pick up this book just to read "Don't make mistakes."

You bought this *particular* book either because you're a fan of *The 2-Hour Job Search* and its emphasis on speed, efficiency, and ease *or* because the cover is really, really good. Either way, you either know now or will come to know that I like to make the job search easier for people rather than harder.

I also recognize that your time and effort are precious resources that I *refuse* to squander. My whole ethos as a career coach is to give job seekers straightforward frameworks that work fast and work well.

Thus, in the remainder of this chapter I will teach you how to make improvements on the Basic Resume to create a Good Resume and then a Great Resume. The Good Resume is designed to work well enough for most job seekers most of the time while requiring *as little time and effort as possible* to prepare. In other words, it is the 80/20 of resumes.

What is 80/20?

Fans of *2HJS* may recall the 80/20 rule—also known as the Pareto principle, after Italian economist Vilfredo Pareto—which states that in most systems one derives 80 percent of their benefit from just 20 percent of their effort. That is effectively what the Good Resume strives for.

The Great Resume, although better than the Good Resume for reasons you will soon see, simply isn't an advisable goal for most, given the additional time and effort required and the limited incremental value; getting a real person to like you enough to actually read your resume is a far more pressing matter, so the Great Resume in most cases is overkill.

Can you summarize these resume types for me?

Absolutely. We'll work through this resumes table in a moment, but as you can see, the one thing all three of the resume types have in common is that they must be error-free.

	BASIC RESUME	GOOD RESUME	GREAT RESUME
Formatting	Error-free	Error-free	Error-free
Bullet Source	Job description	Annual review	"Greatest hits"
Bullets Describe Your ...	Responsibilities	Major projects	Impact (and root causes, if any)
Results Are ...	Not addressed	Provided when quantitative	Always provided

Keep in mind that the Basic Resume has been adequate for decades.

Resume creation is not a skill taught in school, and even if it were, it would likely consist of outdated information like "your resume is your first impression."

In fact, one of the first changes I pushed for when I became a career coach in 2005 was to *de*-emphasize the amount of time we spent on resumes at Duke. It was work most of the coaches found tedious and low-value anyway, and there was never any finish line since every coach could always find a way to improve any resume in their own opinion. This whole time, though, the only time employers *ever* mentioned resumes to us was when they contained errors.

Indeed, employers never contacted our office to complain that students' action verbs were too weak or that results weren't quantified enough. It was always objective errors. Typos. Wonky margins. Mismatched fonts. In other words, they only complained when job seekers couldn't even produce a clean Basic Resume!

I figured that if employers weren't even going to bother complaining about subjective content (bullets), why were we spending so much time trying to improve them? Wouldn't it be rational to just address the errors that recruiters actually cared strongly enough about to highlight?

So we did.

Employers didn't notice.

By making this change, we saved ourselves dozens of painful resume review hours and students saved themselves several frustratingly circular resume revisions. Furthermore, this change actually led to *fewer* employer complaints about resumes, so it was a conclusive win for all parties. By limiting our focus to just what was causing pain to our customers (employers), we increased their satisfaction and decreased student discomfort. Less effort, same results. 80/20.

So do you just not teach your students how to write bullets at all?

Rest assured, all of our students are indeed taught to write effective bullets, just as you will be shortly. However, before we talk effective bullets, we need to talk about some bigger-picture items, like how much time you should spend on creating your resume, what format to use, how long it should be, and so on.

OK, so how much time should I spend on my resume?

My longtime supervisor at Duke, Ed Bernier, has a wonderful rule of thumb with which I fully agree. He tells our students, "Your job search will probably take you about a hundred hours; your resume should take no more than three of them." I call this Ed's Three-Hour Rule.

Thus, three hours.

Three hours? That can't be right. Why is so much attention given to preparing a resume?

On that question we are both bewildered.

But if I had to guess, I think it's a combination of a couple of factors. First, although online job postings quickly diminished the importance of resumes, I think career professionals and job seekers have been slow to change in response.

Career coaches dating all the way back to the late 1900s have been sought out primarily for resume assistance, since resumes alone were once sufficient for getting interviews, pre-online job postings. Today, online postings have *commoditized* resumes—there are simply too many for employers to read through—so suddenly a nice resume isn't enough (or even recognized); to score an interview, you need a perfect background or a referral.

However, when you're a hammer, everything looks like a nail.

For decades, career professionals had made their mark with their ability to prepare resumes. Change is hard! Especially when career coaches had already invested dozens of hours and thousands of dollars securing certifications attesting to the importance of resumes and their ability to create good ones.

But it's not just career coaches. Job *seekers* still expect resume work to both happen first and be critically important, so it's hard to blame professional resume reviewers for filling a real market demand! Old habits die hard, and we prefer the devil we know to the devil we don't: networking, job seekers' biggest boogeyman.

I've spoken to a number of career coaches who *do* recognize the diminished importance of resumes today, but despite that, resume work still constitutes the majority of their business.

That brings us to the second reason. Resumes continue to be heavily emphasized because they give job seekers two critical *perverse incentives*.

What are perverse incentives?

Perverse incentives are an economic term for situations in which desired actions have undesirable results. Perverse incentives are also sometimes referred to as the *cobra effect*, named after this historical example.

During British rule of colonial India, the government wished to reduce the number of cobras and thus offered a bounty for each dead cobra turned in to the government.

You may be able to guess what happened next.

People began to *raise* cobras in order to later turn them in for the bounty money.

The British government caught on to this scheme and, exasperated, eliminated the bounties. As a result, citizens no longer had an incentive to raise cobras, so they released them back into the wild. The net result was *more* cobras rather than less. Thus the cobra effect.[2]

The perverse incentives CVs provide are the illusion of control and a reason to delay. You likely feel powerless when job searching, given that online job posting applications are black holes and results so rarely correlate with the amount of effort expended. The resume is the one part of your job search process that *you* control.

However, I too frequently see job seekers use their resumes as an excuse to delay the scarier, more important part of the search: namely, networking. The thought of networking—asking strangers for help (which requires admitting that the process is outside their control)—terrifies them, so they want to ensure that their CV is *perfect* before putting themselves in a situation where they can (and will) get rejected.

They do tend to continue applying online during this resume revision period, interestingly, effectively choosing certain rejection from machines over possible rejection from people.

In short, stop obsessing over your resume. You will always find a flaw. That is what makes Ed's Three-Hour Rule so useful—it puts a hard stop on your resume work. If you earnestly try to get to Good Resume status, but three hours later all you have to show for it is an error-free Basic Resume, go with that!

However, most of you should be able to secure at least Good Resume status in three hours, so let's make that our goal.

What resume format should I use?

Again, ask ten different career coaches, get ten different opinions, but while there is no consensus on a "best resume template," there is some agreement that resumes should be easy to read, and that usually means breaking up your resume with headers and featuring some white space.

I am passionate about removing the barriers to job searching, so rather than create a proprietary resume template for you to download (further raising the profile of a document I very much want you to de-emphasize), I offer you a template you likely already have access to— namely, the "Resume (chronological)" template in Microsoft Word—as a starting point.

To find this template in Word, as of this printing (and depending on your version), navigate to File > New and in the "Search for online templates" box, enter "Resume (chronological)." You should get one that looks roughly like the following. (And if you can't because the template is renamed or no longer available, please join my LinkedIn Group, "The 2-Hour Job Search Q&A Forum," to learn where you can find a suitable replacement.)

Your Name
Job Title
Contact Info

Objective
...

Skills & Abilities
...

Experience
Company Name, Location   Dates
...

Company Name, Location   Dates
...

Education
School name, location, degree   Dates
...

Communication
...

Leadership
...

To be clear, this template is *not* perfect. Just as there are no perfect resumes, there are no perfect resume templates. In fact, we are going to delete entire sections from this template to make completing our resume go faster, with less effort (don't worry; nobody will miss what we delete).

What I like about this template is that it uses space economically (by placing dates to the *right* of employer name and job title rather than below on a separate line), is clean and easy to read, and will help you get this done quickly without having to worry about additional downloads.

So how do I write the Objective section at the top?

I have good news! We won't write it at all! That's one of the sections we will delete.

Delete the resume's Objective? How will people know what I want?

Again, remember that resumes are no longer an employer's first impression of us. To get a resume seen requires either directly relevant experience or an internal advocate. Hiring managers simply receive too many resumes to spend time wading through each one and looking for diamonds in the rough.

The problem with Objective statements (or their close cousins, Profile statements) is that they are a microcosm of everything wrong with a resume: they require just as much agony and effort on their own as the actual resume itself, but they are done in miniature—in poetry form instead of prose, if you will. Regardless, just like with a resume, all that effort never makes a difference and people are rarely satisfied with the results.

Because job seekers are trying to say a lot in a few words with their Objective and Profile statements, they typically tend to become repositories for buzzwords and clichés, featuring subjective terms like "team player," "hardworking," and "problem solver" that are rather vapid and impossible to substantiate.

Therefore, we will delete that section and save ourselves literally hours of work and anxiety. We'll instead pour that work into networking; *that's* how employers will know what we're looking for.

But I have to have an Objective statement!

If you insist—and again, I discourage this—keep it *objective* (meaning *all facts*, such as "Chemical engineer with budget management experience seeking financial analyst position"), down to one line, and use it primarily to mention the title of the role that you are targeting.

Yes, I realize that mentioning the title of the role you are targeting means you'd need to update your resume every time you send it to a different employer, which is another reason I don't recommend having this on your resume in the first place. Successful job seekers use informational meetings rather than resumes to make first impressions, and to better effect.

Finally, if you spend more than ten minutes trying to create one, recognize that you are overinvesting. I'd say just delete the Objective statement for the time being, finish the rest of the resume first, and then reevaluate whether you *really* still need it once you see how else you might use that space and/or time.

But what about keywords to "beat" applicant tracking systems (ATS)?

Ugh. Before I elaborate, let me first explain what an ATS is.

After online job postings gained popularity and employers suddenly received *too many* applications for a job rather than too few, they realized they had better things to do than read resumes all day. So employers purchased an ATS to help them process all the applications by highlighting those containing desired information (and, ignoring the rest).

Despite the plethora of breathless articles about how critical it is to insert certain words into your resume in order to appease the ATS gods, there is simply no data supporting the idea that this is a good (or even neutral) use of your time.

Imagine for argument's sake that there *was* a magical list of keywords that maximized the chance your resume would be "found" among hundreds of others in a pool of online applicants—wouldn't *everyone* just start using those keywords, rendering them useless?

When hiring managers use an ATS, they are not looking for resumes that used "supervised" rather than "managed"; they are looking for people who have Product Manager in their resume as part of their past experience. Or they are looking for people with a specific degree or credential, like a CPA or the ability to code in Python. Or they are looking for people who worked for their competitor and already understand the industry.

In other words, when they use an ATS they are looking for *objective* criteria, not subjective info. Thus, no matter how you finesse your bullet points, you are unlikely to improve your odds of being picked out by a resume keyword search. Don't play that game. Save yourself the hours of anguish; instead, devote it to meeting smart people who can help you find jobs and learn along the way.

What about the Skills & Abilities section underneath the Objective in that template?

We're going to delete that too! (Isn't making a resume easy?)

These Skills & Abilities sections suffer from the same deficiencies as the Objective and Profile statements. They are like writing poetry, subject to endless wordsmithing and tinkering without ever really finding a satisfying stopping point.

Time and effort aside, anything of value you would otherwise put here (such as programming languages and certifications) will show up elsewhere in your resume, so if an employer does do a keyword search on an objective qualification or job title, yours will be found.

Finally, you're going to need the space for your actual accomplishments, so it's an easy place to save a bunch of lines of space! We'll just jump right into the Experience section. One note before we do: while this type of resume is called "chronological," your experience will actually be presented in reverse chronological order, with your most recent work experiences at the top of the page.

So how long *should* my resume be?

Again, since your resume should never be the first impression an employer has of you, a one-page resume is fine for most everyone these days for anyone outside of academia (and within academia, your CV will definitely be longer and subject to its own unique formatting, given the emphasis on your publications to date). I've literally never looked at a one-page resume and thought, *Where's the rest of it?* Nor have I ever heard a colleague say that, about even very experienced applicants. Instead, we appreciate the brevity.

That said, I would *at the least* expect most people under age thirty-five to get their resume down to one page. Yes, this may involve cutting experiences from earlier in your career, but most people tend to do more impressive versions of projects later in their career anyway. If that is the case for you as well, simply cut the less-impressive versions of similar projects from earlier in your career so your resume is as close as possible to being a "greatest hits" list of bullets rather than a comprehensive list of how all of your professional hours to date were spent, which would bore both you and your prospective employers to tears. Furthermore, in an interview you'll want to talk about your more impressive accomplishments anyway, so why put yourself at risk of getting asked about bullet points highlighting the inferior earlier stories you barely remember?

What do you mean by "at risk"?

Anything you put in your resume is something an interviewer can ask you about. In one interview, my interviewer pointed at one of my bullet points and said, "Tell me about *that* one," and as I walked them through the experience, asked me follow-up questions about my logic and strategy.

Then they did it again.

And again.

Going into more detail on a bullet point is really hard to do when your bullets start with "Responsible for," since those aren't stories, by definition. They are job descriptions, which are tedious to discuss and don't show you in your best light. Therefore, our bullet points will be *accomplishment statements* rather than *responsibility statements*.

What is an accomplishment statement?

An accomplishment statement is a description of the impact you made with the responsibilities you held, rather than just the responsibilities themselves. This is the key factor that differentiates Good and Great Resumes from Basic Resumes.

Basic Resumes feature responsibility statements in their bullet points, which often are language pulled directly from the job description (see the *Bullet Source* column in the table on page 33). Responsibility statements typically start with passive phrasing like "responsible for" or "in charge of," and verbs like "oversaw," "coordinated," "assisted with," or "collaborated on" and the bullets describe responsibilities and theoretical duties rather than actual actions taken.

Basic Resume language has been considered adequate for decades, but it is simple to improve, and those improvements will set you up much, much better to interview later on. The first way to move on from Basic Resume responsibility statements to Good Resume accomplishment statements is to get specific. Instead of talking about what you were *supposed* to do generally, discuss what you *actually did* specifically—the projects you'd list on an annual review, and the key actions taken to complete them.

Great Resumes improve on Good Resumes by clarifying *why* each bullet is impressive. Here's how this all looks in practice:

- Responsible for refrigerated biscuit marketing budget of $400 million **(BASIC RESUME)**
- Analyzed advertising channels to optimally allocate $400 million marketing budget **(GOOD RESUME)**
- Optimized $400 million marketing budget by analyzing historical returns and increasing budget to highest-return channel (newspaper inserts), increasing profits by 22 percent **(GREAT RESUME)**

You'll notice that Great Resume bullet points will tend to be longer than Basic and Good Resume bullet points, simply because it takes more words to cite specific actions and the impact achieved. This is totally appropriate.

Great Resumes will have fewer bullet points, but they'll all be of higher quality. Furthermore, by featuring fewer bullet points, you can ensure that only the best of your best accomplishments are "at risk" of being asked about in an interview. That's perfect, since those are the ones you'll want to discuss anyway.

In this example, you are not obligated to mention that you reallocated that budget every year for the three years you held that role; instead, just highlight the one time you managed that budget *best*. By getting specific—both about the particular iteration of a project you did most effectively *and* what specific insights you had that enabled exceptional results (like the newspaper inserts mentioned in the example)—you make the accomplishment both more memorable and more credible.

One other thing you may notice about Great Resume bullet points is that they *always* include impact. Accomplishment statements (like the one in the Great Resume example) don't stop with responsibilities (as in Basic Resumes) or projects (as in Good Resumes)—they finish with results. What exceptional results did you *achieve* with those responsibilities and opportunities?

That seems easy when your projects feature numbers, but what if my projects don't?

You should always include results if you want to have a Great Resume, but that doesn't mean all of your results must be quantified *numerically*.

Maybe you don't think your projects had any impact, but your previous employers *paid you* to do them, so they must have carried some importance. Perhaps your efforts didn't increase sales or profit in a measurable way, but did they:

- Reduce risk?
- Improve efficiency?
- Simplify tasks?
- Increase knowledge?

Similarly, if you don't have exact numbers, you can use approximations instead, such as "efforts to streamline expense reporting cut errors by half and reduced reconciliation time from days to hours."

I'm still freaked out about this results thing. Can I just not feature results?

Absolutely.

Probably not what you were expecting me to say, right?

Truly, Basic Resumes—even substandard ones where there *are* typos and formatting issues—have been the norm since they gained mainstream popularity in the 1950s,[3] so if it feels like adding results (even qualitative ones like the ones just listed) to your bullet points would take you an extra ten hours, *don't do it.* It's simply not worth it. Just make sure it's error-free.

That's the trap of obsessing over your resume. The more time you spend wordsmithing profile statements and bullet points, and the longer your resume gets in the hopes that a prospective hiring manager (or, more realistically, an ATS) will spot *some*thing they find inspiring enough to invite you to interview, the higher the probability that your resume will feature an error of some sort. Your eyes become numb to your own resume after staring at it for so long, and the more words your resume contains, the more chances you have to mess things up.

So don't stress about results if that's what's going to keep you from moving forward with your job search. In fact, if you are *certain* that your Basic Resume is error-free, then go with that and stop tinkering.

Each time you change something, you're reintroducing the chance of errors. So unless you consider that change important enough to warrant another round of error-checking with software or friends whose eyes aren't *also* numb to your resume by this point, don't do it.

Wait—there are software programs that can check for errors?

Yes, there are! Microsoft Word will help you catch *most* typos, misspellings, and some grammar issues, and a free tool called Grammarly will do the same for both your word-processing software (Word, for most of us) and email services. And many business schools, Duke included, are big fans of a tool called VMock, a resume-specific analysis tool that is also free for individual users. No tool is perfect, but that's part of the reason we don't want to mess with our resumes any more than we have to once we are confident they are error-free.

All that said, I find these supplemental tools are most useful, again, for helping you catch *objective* errors rather than for improving *subjective* content. VMock will, for example, point out if you've used the same action words over and over and suggest replacements and will highlight the use of jargon and filler words (like "successfully"—you're probably not going to list projects on which you failed, right?) for removal, which is helpful as well.

Just don't get lost in all of the analytics about skills demonstrated and how your resume scores compare to others. Simply use a tool for what it's intended to focus on: identifying errors that even conscientious human readers might miss.

What if the only results I can find are my entire team's, and my work was just a small piece of that effort?

Great question! Here is where I have a couple of favorite hedging (or qualifying) phrases: "contributing to" and "helping to." Both can precede any results you cite to show that your efforts were part of a larger effort, but still imply that your efforts were instrumental in achieving that result.

So what about the Education section? Do I delete that too?

Nope! That one's a keeper. If you are currently in a program or recently graduated, I'd recommend moving this up to the first position, before your Experience section.

You can list your GPA, extracurriculars, awards, exchange programs, and more here, but keep these at one to two lines underneath your school and major.

What do I do with the Communication and Leadership headers?

Replace Leadership with Additional Information—that's a must-have, for reasons I will explain shortly—and either delete the Communication section entirely or replace it with a more useful header based on your circumstances.

What other headers should I consider?

The most common ones I recommend are Entrepreneurial Experience and Community Experience. (If you use either of those, you would retitle your Experience section as Work Experience or Professional Experience, to differentiate the two.)

The Entrepreneurial Experience header is a good idea if you've started your own business in tandem with your other work experience.

This way, your better-recognized employer names still appear at the top of your resume, while your own enterprise garners special attention lower down. (TheLadders.com's eye-tracking study showed that items immediately following headers get more attention than those in the middle.)

The one caveat to this advice is if you had quit your other job(s) to pursue your entrepreneurial venture full time. This may make it seem as if you have a gap in your work history, which makes some hiring managers very nervous (although I think this nervousness is outdated and silly—many of us have had experiences with layoffs or taking time off to care for or start a family).

Thus, proceed with caution if this describes your situation. (Also, I recommend describing your work experience in years *only*—no months. This will make some employment gaps disappear altogether, while making your resume easier to read overall.)

The Community Experience header is good for job seekers who may lack much paid work experience but who have taken on leadership roles serving their communities. Treat these bullets just as you would any others. Focus on the instances your volunteerism created exceptional impact (when possible) not just hours served. Remember, *resumes are for your "greatest hits," not your average days.*

So what about this Additional Information section you mentioned?

Additional Information actually *does* get looked at, so it's kind of important!

It's the one part of a resume that makes you seem like a real person instead of a theoretical concept. It also serves a very real function: the information you include here will often be the subject of the small talk an interviewer initiates with you at the start of a job interview, should you successfully land one, so you want to include information that not only professionally informs but also builds rapport.

What do you mean by "professionally informs"?

This includes any other salient information that informs the employer about your ability to do the work for which you are putting yourself forward. So this is the place to list relevant certifications, languages (both programming and spoken), volunteer or entrepreneurial experience (if you didn't split it out as a separate section), work authorization (where relevant), and the like.

For this information, I recommend putting each different topic on a separate line, starting each line with a bolded title (like "**Programming languages:**" or "**Community service:**"). Keep this Additional Information section to no more than five lines of content.

What about information that builds rapport?

This can include a line about "Hobbies:" or "Travel:" or both, or any other subject that will help an employer get to know you more holistically (such as "Competitive running:" followed by a list of races you've completed or highlights or awards you've earned). Play it safe here, though. Be wary of controversial topics such as political and religious affiliations, since they will alienate at least some readers, either because they don't share your beliefs or they don't feel they are appropriate to mention in your CV.

Either way, make sure you have at least one or two lines that focus on personally meaningful, rapport-building topics you enjoy speaking about. Having more is fine, as long as all relevant professional information fits within your five-line limit.

Is there anything else I can do now that will help set me up for interviews later?

Yes, there absolutely is!

Since each bullet point on your resume represents a story you need to be prepared to tell in an interview, start creating a spreadsheet where you list each story in its own row. This is the start of what we'll call our CAR (Challenge-Action-Result) Matrix. CAR is the industry standard format for answering so-called behavioral interview questions, which tend to begin with phrases like "Tell me about a time when you . . ." or "Give me an example of when you . . ."

We'll discuss interviewing in more detail later, but start your story brainstorming now. In chapter 6 we will fill in the columns of your CAR Matrix with interview questions we have been (or expect to be) asked, like

"Give me an example of when you led without formal authority" or "Tell me about a time when you changed your supervisor's mind."

If you are struggling to identify bullets for your resume, you may wish to skip ahead to chapter 6 to see some commonly asked interview questions. The stories that come to mind may spark additional bullet ideas while also preparing you for interviews.

This approach also helps you avoid double work. Too often I see novice job seekers spend dozens of hours wordsmithing Basic Resume responsibility statements, only to need to brainstorm actual accomplishments later anyway (since CAR stories must be more specific than just job duties).

Instead, write accomplishment statements for your bullets *now*—either in a CAR Matrix or directly into your resume—so you don't have to do it *later*.

So I'm supposed to get all this done in three hours?

No! You are supposed to get as much of this done as you *can* in three hours before moving on, keeping in mind that if it takes you three hours to achieve an error-free Basic Resume, that should suffice. However, I find that most job seekers find writing accomplishment statements no more challenging or painful than writing responsibility statements!

If it's going to be tedious either way, you might as well write the good kind of bullets instead of the bad kind.

CHAPTER CHECKLIST	
Are you *certain* your resume is error free? (Basic Resume)	✓
If so, are your bullet points accomplishment statements rather than responsibility statements? (Good Resume)	✓
If so, do you provide results for every bullet point? (Great Resume)	✓

TROUBLESHOOTING

I can't think of any accomplishments—how do I identify them?

First, think smaller. Neither bullet points nor interview stories cover years-long projects.

Typically, good bullets will cover work that ranges in duration from a day to several months. Projects lasting a year or more should probably be split into multiple bullets. Nearly all projects have a research phase at the beginning, a strategy phase in the middle, and an implementation phase at the end (we'll cover this in more detail in chapter 6), so if you discuss each of those phases as their own stories, often you can turn one multiyear project responsibility bullet into two or three more impactful accomplishment statements.

Second, review the interview questions presented in chapter 6. Sometimes seeing specific behavioral interview questions will spark memories of professional experiences you've had that may lend themselves well to bullets, preventing you from having to brainstorm these experiences later and enabling you to use your resume as a cheat sheet for the stories you're prepared to tell once in an interview.

Third, and finally, if you haven't already done so, take the StrengthsFinder test and review your results. That test will highlight some skills that have in the past provided natural venues for you to excel. Was your top talent theme Command? If so, you probably have a great accomplishment statement about influencing a group. Was it Communication? If so, you probably have (time and time again) found ways to make complicated things easy for others to understand, to great effect.

There won't be one right answer for everyone, but I find these three to be the most helpful in the least amount of time!

I spent three hours on my resume and I'm still on my first bullet point—what do I do?

First, take a deep breath. Resumes are intimidating. Furthermore, your entire support network has probably made you really paranoid about the faux-importance of resumes.

Don't let them. The only thing people agree on with resumes is that they should be error-free and easy to read, but beyond that, beauty is in the eye of the beholder.

If you are just completely stuck, I recommend that you aim for Good Resume status. Look through your past annual reviews, to see which projects were worthy of mention, and summarize the cleverest actions you took to complete those projects. If you don't have access to annual reviews and can't wrap your head around the accomplishment statement concept at all, simply open your old job descriptions and pull language from those to create your bullets.

Again, bullets (like resumes themselves) simply don't have a very big impact. No single bullet is going to get you noticed by an employer—only a relevant previous job title or elite pedigree can do that—so relax and do your best.

Once you've done your best, upload your resume draft into a resume analysis tool such as VMock to see what suggestions *it* has for you. If you agree, incorporate them. If you disagree, stick to your guns. Just make sure you've fixed any objective errors before proceeding, and you'll be OK.

We have bigger fish to fry than resumes, after all!

CHAPTER 3

LinkedIn Profile

Do I need to pay for a LinkedIn Premium account?

No! A lot of people do—I think it's a combination of FOMO (fear of miss-ing out) and the fact that everybody loves a free month of anything (LinkedIn's "first month free" of Premium membership is the stuff of legend)—but there's really no need. Everything you will need to do on LinkedIn, you will be able to do for free.

In fact, with the exception of the StrengthsFinder test I recommended in chapter 1, *everything* I recommend to you in this book will be free.

In general, I find it's best to be wary of anyone who says you have to spend money to make money.

So what do I need to do on LinkedIn?

It would be *very* easy for me to say "you need to do *everything*"—nobody would criticize me for telling you to check all of the boxes that LinkedIn sets out for you, no matter the time it takes—but that's not really how I work. You and I both know you're not going to live forever, so we need to get this done and move on to more impactful efforts.

I think your LinkedIn profile is another 80/20 exercise. You could spend ages chasing recommendations and endorsements and adding more and more connections, but in my experience none of those make a predictable impact.

So back to your question: what do I think you genuinely *need* to do in your LinkedIn profile? Not a whole lot. Therefore, in this chapter I'll walk you through, section by section, to tell you which you need to focus on and which you can skip.

Overall, we'll adopt a mind-set very similar to what we have for our resume—objectively perfect, subjectively good enough. (Just as with resumes, no two people will agree on what a perfect LinkedIn profile looks like, either.)

However, for most professions you will need to at least *have* a LinkedIn profile, since that's how many employers will look up your work history.

But won't employers already have a copy of my resume?

If you've reached the interview stage of an employer's process, then yes, but even then, many employers would still rather see your LinkedIn profile than your resume.

Why is that?

All LinkedIn profiles are in the *exact* same format regardless of what schools you attended or for which previous employers you worked, making it easier for a viewer to skim them to find the information they are seeking.

So does that mean I should just recreate my resume in LinkedIn?

Thankfully, that's not necessary. Remember, what employers are typically looking for on LinkedIn is your *objective* experience: job titles held, employers worked for, schools attended, and certifications and degrees attained.

If you include this information and only this information, you will have achieved the Basic Resume level of proficiency in LinkedIn, minus just two pieces: a professional-looking headshot for your profile and a headline.

What if I can't afford a professional headshot?

Just ask any photography-fanatic friend to take a picture of you on their iPhone or preferred camera. It truly is remarkable, the camera quality that travels in pockets and purses these days. Your face, but not your background, should be in focus; the iPhone's Portrait mode makes this incredibly simple. Take your headshot in front of a solid background or outside just before sunset (so the sun is neither too harsh nor too dark—as a paler person myself, I prefer this time deemed "golden hour" by photographers because it gives everything a warm and tanned glow). LinkedIn now offers several filters for the headshots you upload, which you can use to put your best face forward.

Furthermore, wear the clothes you would expect to wear if hired for your desired role, and get a variety of shots from the elbows up as well as more tightly framed on your face so you have some options. You can always crop the wider shots to just your face if you spot a wrinkle in your shirt, but you can't zoom great shots out any wider than they were taken.

You want to appear approachable, so don't be formal—relax and smile.

What should I do for my headline?

This presents the same risks as the Objective and Profile statements in resumes—it can take you hours and hours to come up with something you're never fully satisfied with. However, unlike with a resume, you *must* have a headline in LinkedIn, so we need to quickly come up with something good enough.

The easiest version of a good-enough headline—provided you are not seeking to change careers—is an *objective* description of the experience you've had to date. The simplest version of this is just your current job title and employer. If that's your situation, just write "Associate Marketing Manager with General Mills" and call it a day! Similarly, if you're a current student, cite your school, major, and graduation date and complete this section quickly. These headlines won't garner accolades, but they won't scare anyone off either and they can be created in a fraction of the time a more creative headline would take.

If you're unemployed or seeking to switch careers, things get a bit trickier.

Let's tackle the unemployed case first. In *2HJS*, I emphasize the importance of not appearing desperate. You want to give yourself options, since options help you organically convey to employers that you are the type of job seeker who has options. Unfortunately, aspirational headlines like "Seeking new opportunity in product management" or "Aspiring real estate professional seeking next role" don't effectively convey confidence. In fact, I think they communicate the opposite. What to do, then?

My favorite approach here is a broad description of you as a professional in fifteen words or less. It could be one phrase or a collection of descriptors.

That sounds great in theory, but what do these look like in practice?

Here are some sample concepts to spur your imagination:

- Empathetic health care professional focused on treating minds *and* bodies
- Growth catalyst and project management expert
- Making nonprofits work better, one mission at a time
- Brand Builder | Project Leader | Consumer Whisperer
- Creative problem solver who turns big obstacles into small ones

The key is, don't agonize over this. I recommend writing down a lot of phrases that you *might* use just to see which ones resonate with you, rather than trying to come up with a good headline on your first try. In fact, if you're in this situation, do it right now. Take the next minute and just start writing or typing phrases that are ownable and unique to you. (Revisiting your How Your Talents Add Value exercise from chapter 1 may help you in this effort; see page 17.)

The good news is that this doesn't need to be done all at once, so if none of the phrases you just came up with resonate with you, set it aside for now—you may have a moment of inspiration on your walk into the supermarket. Hopefully, you can see from the preceding examples that these are not Pulitzer-worthy. It's really just something that (1) does *not* advertise you are looking for a job and (2) gives people a sense of who you are and what you are about.

One word of caution before we leave headlines: please don't regress to clichés, jargon, and generalities—you don't want your headline sounding like the Summary or Profile statement I just discouraged you from including in your resume!

If you include authentic phrases that are true to you rather than phrases you think a potential employer wants to hear, you'll be fine. Just as with resumes, employers who are already looking at your LinkedIn profile are predisposed to like you—why else did they just take the time to call up *your* profile rather than one of the other 575 million profiles out there? So pick something adequate to start, and iterate when you think of phrases that describe you better.

How do I tackle the About section?

This one always struck me as a longer version of your headline, but with less visibility. It's the perfect example of something that nobody will miss if it's not there, so leaving it blank is totally an option. That said, most people will have *some*thing here to summarize their *objective* experience to date. If you're not sure of what to put here, keep it pretty short. A line or two summarizing your background and experience will suffice, especially if that information wasn't already mentioned in your headline.

On the other hand, if you have more to write and using this section feels authentic to you, give it a shot, but note that the risk here is that it gets so long that nobody wants to read it (and, again, it's not going to be something that gets you "found," so best to minimize your investment here).

Just note that obsessing over your About section is *not* an excuse to delay networking. It is a doom loop, just like pursuing endlessly clashing resume expert reviews. Just accept that your About section will never be perfect; it will just eat up as much time as you give to it. And in this book, we are focused strictly on getting to networking as quickly as possible without doing ourselves any material harm (and actually adding a lot of value along the way, too), so let's keep moving!

What about the Experience section?

Yes, this one is sort of important! However, it's important in the same way the resume is important. It's an error-free way to communicate your *objective* career information; anything beyond that is gravy.

Thus, if you (as I do) just put your employers, job titles, and dates of employment, you won't win any awards but you also won't do yourself any harm, and you'll complete this section in just a handful of minutes.

The lovely thing about LinkedIn is that it is an *abridged* resume. It gives you the information you want to know in a predictable format, and if you want to read (or write) more, the option is there. However, I've never heard an employer critique a candidate for not having a fully replicated resume or entirely new content in their LinkedIn profile, nor have I ever heard that the employer was expecting *additional* information over what was in the resume.

So, from an efficiency perspective, I think you have three options:

1. Include *only* objective information (employers, job titles, locations, and employment dates).

2. Include *select* bullets from your resume (the one you put at the top is usually your best one, so feel free to go with that).

3. Fully replicate your resume in your LinkedIn profile (but use the same language, to avoid double work).

Pick whichever approach feels most natural to you, but again, don't fall into the quagmire of trying to create new and original content for LinkedIn. Your (error-free) objective content is what's important. Other things beyond that are nice to have if your time and aptitude allow, but I strongly advise taking full advantage of the work you already did on your resume's bullet points—or just leaving them out entirely to make your profile even easier to read.

And the Education section?

Very similar deal here. The facts of your education are what count: schools attended, degrees earned, and areas of particular study. Note that including your dates of graduation is totally optional. More experienced professionals may wish to omit graduation dates to avoid the risk of ageism in their search.

If you did not already mention info about your formative educational extracurriculars in your About section, feel free to include those here. That being said, if you leave blank the descriptions underneath your school(s) attended, nobody will bat an eye. You will be just fine and save yourself a lot of work.

What about the Licenses & Certifications section?

If you have them, include them here. If not, skip this section entirely.

And the Volunteer Experience section?

I also consider this section optional, although if you have limited professional experience and/or had a community or volunteer experience section in your resume, this will bolster your years of experience and give people a sense of the causes that are important to you and demonstrate (if applicable) that you have taken leadership roles in addressing them.

Now what about the Skills & Endorsements section?

These are pretty meaningless. Honestly, I've never seen someone benefit from having many nor suffer for having few. It does, however, drive traffic on LinkedIn's site—be it to ask for Skills & Endorsements, write them for other people, and so on—so it's great for them.

Thus, don't take this section too seriously. It, too, can be a time suck without adding value, but in general it causes no harm.

Let me guess—same with the Recommendations section?

You bet. Again, these are nice to have (and really flattering!), but they won't systematically improve your odds of getting an interview or being found by hiring managers.

They can, however, turn into the LinkedIn version of holiday cards: you may not want to send them, but you send them anyway because you know other people are going to send them to you. "I'll write you one if you write me one," forgetting that few people are going to be reading this far down into your profile unless they already liked you anyway.

So skip them for now. This section is something you can always seek out or do for others when time permits, but I assume you're reading this book because you are job searching imminently. If that's the case, this is an easy one to pass on for the moment. Get a few more hours of sleep instead.

What about Accomplishments? And Interests? And so on . . . ?

Nobody will miss these if they are not there, plain and simple.

That said, look through the options for low-hanging fruit! If you have Awards, Publications, foreign language abilities, and the like, list them! Just don't spend much time here. Simply list the objective information that's easy to include, and save the subjective information or items requiring explanation for after your networking efforts are already under way.

So a professional photo, a serviceable Headline, my just-the-facts Experience and Education info, and that's it?

Indeed. The rest is great if you have the time, energy, and wherewithal, but your MVP LinkedIn profile can feature just those items you listed. Not so bad, right? That leaves us plenty of time to address cover letters, and then we can start talking about the interviews themselves!

Are you *certain* your LinkedIn profile is error-free?	✓
Do you have a professional (or professional-looking) headshot?	✓
Do you have an authentic Headline of fifteen words or less?	✓
Do you have your objective information listed (employers, job titles, dates of employment, and schools attended)?	✓

TROUBLESHOOTING

Something you said in this chapter doesn't match what I'm seeing on LinkedIn—what gives?

LinkedIn frequently changes their interface—usually about once a year, with more serious facelifts every several years—so it is likely some of this information may fall out of date at some point.

I run a LinkedIn Group called The 2-Hour Job Search—Q&A Forum where I will address any format changes that you may experience and give you recommendations for how to best account for them. The LinkedIn Group is absolutely free, so you're welcome to join as a full participant or just to lurk and see if you find anything interesting.

Furthermore, the LinkedIn Group is where I post updates whenever my recommended frameworks change (like flannel sheets, my approaches improve with each use—suggestions from both my students and readers like you have become new parts of the canon!), so please join the group, share your results, ask questions, and help others facing similar situations. The more, the merrier!

CHAPTER 4

Cover Letters

Aren't there *entire books* devoted to how to write a perfect cover letter? What makes you think you can tell me how to do it in twelve pages?

It starts with acknowledging that *there is no such thing as a perfect cover letter.*

Déjà vu, right?

The good news is that cover letters are *far* more interesting than resumes. They illustrate how well you can construct an argument (when responding to the question "Why should we consider *you*?" specifically). The cover letter informs the employer about your knowledge of the role and how your skills make you well suited for it. Furthermore, it offers insight into your communication skills.

As you can tell, I'm a big fan of cover letters. It's a free writing sample! Say I'm the hiring manager. In a single page, it tells me whether I'd want to get project update emails from this person. Are they the type of employee that will include everything *they* want me to know (like all the work they put into this project), or are they the type who'll tell me what *I*, the hiring manager, want and need to know?

Plus, I am going to give you a framework that makes writing cover letters a snap. Gone are the days where you would write 450 words in the hopes that a recruiter would find thirty of them helpful. We are going to go in the other direction, imagining that this cover letter is an email to our boss's boss. It's going to be short, to the point, authentic, customer-focused, error-free, and done.

Yeah, that sounds great, but *how*?

In this chapter, I will introduce you to the RAC (Reason-Anecdote-Connection) Model, a framework we'll use again later during interviews to answer "Why?" questions (like "Why our company?" or "Why this role?").

Again, I consider the cover letter itself to be answering a "Why?" question—namely, "Why should we consider *you*?" You won't often hear that rather combative question in interviews, but consider it the prompt to which you are responding whenever you are writing a cover letter.

When exactly will I be writing a cover letter?

There are two specific occasions—facilitated and unfacilitated—and we'll cover both cases.

First, we'll tackle the case you've probably already got in mind: the unfacilitated cover letter. By unfacilitated, I mean the kind you submit with a resume to an online job posting rather than to a person who has requested that you do so.

You should not be writing many unfacilitated cover letters.

The exception to this rule is if you are currently in an academic program where job postings are made available to you. Although your career center facilitated the opportunity in the first place, I would still consider the cover letter you write for these to be unfacilitated, since your cover letter will be judged vis-à-vis your classmates' merits rather than on its own. If you have access to a career center's job postings, then you will likely be writing *many* unfacilitated cover letters. However, once you no longer have access to a career center, you should write far fewer, relying instead on the advocates you develop to make the case for you.

In *those* cases, either you'll be asked to write a short (facilitated) cover letter in an email and attach your resume so they can simply forward it along to the hiring manager or human resources *or* you'll be exempted from having to write a cover letter altogether. (For real. Having advocates is the best!)

But first things first—let's address the case you likely picked up this book for, before tackling the one you didn't realize was a thing until about three hundred words ago!

Fine. Then how do I write an unfacilitated cover letter?

The RAC Model I mentioned earlier creates short, impactful cover letters in just 200 to 300 words. For simplicity's sake, we'll call these cover letters RAC Letters to differentiate them from cover letters following other formats (or no format).

Essentially, a RAC Letter is a five-paragraph cover letter with an introductory paragraph, three RAC paragraphs in which you systematically detail why you think you'd be a good fit, and a short closing paragraph asking for an interview and providing contact info. That's really it.

Now let's take a detailed look at each of these paragraph types in turn.

So what do I write in the introductory paragraph of a RAC Letter?

Simply state the position you're interested in, any key advocates you have at that organization, and an expression of belief that you can add value to the employer "in the following ways," which will lead you into your RAC paragraphs. Optionally, you can choose to include any single story, reason, or major motivation you may have that relates to why *this* position and why *now*.

Don't try to do too much here—again, imagine this is an email that is going to your future boss's boss, so you want to keep it lean and mean.

What about the RAC paragraphs?

In each, you'll state a skill or attribute (a Reason—note that for brevity I'll use this capitalized "Reason" to mean "skill or attribute" for the remainder of this book) that you think would make you appealing to the employer. This doesn't even need to be a full sentence. In fact, I recommend simply making this a bolded word or short phrase followed by a colon, like "**Leadership:**" or "**Comfort with ambiguity:**".

Your next sentence will provide them an Anecdote that illustrates why you think the employer should find your Reason *true* or *important*. The Anecdote can take a few forms:

- A *brief* summary of a bullet point on your resume that illustrates that skill or attribute (in more natural language than appears on your resume, mind you!)

- A story about earning an accolade or award by demonstrating proficiency at that Reason

- Information you learned—perhaps from online research or someone you spoke to in an informational meeting—that reinforces the importance of that Reason within their organization and/or similar ones

In the first two examples, the Anecdote is proof that you possess that skill or attribute (in other words, your Reason is *true*). In the third, your Anecdote is proof that your Reason matters to the employer (your Reason is *important*). The fact that the Anecdote can take one of two forms is a bit confusing, I realize, but either form serves your purpose: it lets the employer know you don't make sweeping assertions without support; instead, you back up your arguments with proof.

Finally, if you'd like to and if word count allows—or if your Reason's benefit to the employer is not immediately obvious—you'll finish with one sentence that connects (Connection) your Reason to something the employer cares about. Will your skill increase sales? Decrease errors? Make the teams you're on work better together? Allow you to derive better insight from data analysis?

This sentence is where you demonstrate that you understand the job you're applying for and appreciate that the employer—not you—is the ultimate audience of this cover letter.

Connecting resume bullets to cover letters

Think of your resume bullets as a list of ingredients and your cover letter as a free sample of the dish you'd prepare *from* those ingredients. Use the cover letter to add color and flavor by better establishing the degree of difficulty of a particular accomplishment or by positioning yourself as *uniquely* qualified, knowledgeable, or motivated in a specific area, rather than just proficient.

For example, recall the Great Resume bullet point example from chapter 2 (see page 41): "Optimized $400 million marketing budget by analyzing historical returns and increasing budget to highest-return channel (newspaper inserts), increasing profits by 22 percent." With a few additional words you can increase the impact of that accomplishment, like this: "**Analytical skills:** As the youngest-ever Marketing Manager at FormerEmployer.com, I increased profits by 22 percent by identifying our most productive marketing channel and convincing a wary management team to shift a greater portion of our advertising budget toward it."

Commentary, such as clarifying that you were the youngest Marketing Manager in the company or that management was not immediately supportive of the idea, might be too subjective (that is, based on your own personal opinion) to appear in a bullet point. However, in cover letters, such context is totally appropriate and adds helpful texture to cover letter RACs for clarifying why your Reason is valid.

So make your words *count*. Refrain from the common temptation of using your cover letter's greater word count to add additional "whats": descriptions of what your previous employer's business model was or what your department's role or duties were. Instead, emphasize *why* your accomplishment was especially meaningful.

So what should my three Reasons be?

Yeah, about that . . .

This question is inevitable, but in practice I find job seekers frequently spend *way* too much time thinking about what the *right* Reasons are and way too little time on clarifying why that Reason is specific to *them* as a candidate (their Anecdote) or why the employer should care (their Connection). There simply aren't "correct" Reasons to put in *any* cover letter.

Nearly every other job seeker who also sends an unfacilitated cover letter will likely pick qualities straight from the job description and speak to those. I don't think this is a terrible approach—in fact, it's one of the two I'd recommend! However, most job seekers who don't use a RAC Model tend to drone on and on, restating bullets from their resume with more detail but without any additional application to the employer or description of why a particular accomplishment was especially challenging or impressive.

Even if the job description explicitly states the employer wants candidates to stress three particular qualities in their cover letters (in which case I'd definitely recommend making those your three Reasons), if you use the RAC Model to concisely develop your Reasons with Anecdotes and then Connect them back to the employer's needs, you will dramatically and favorably differentiate your cover letter.

The alternative to picking the three Reasons you think the employer most wants to see is to pick the three Reasons that would *make* you the best candidate. In the marketing world, we'd call these *points of differentiation* rather than *points of parity*.

What are points of parity and points of differentiation?

Points of parity are elements that everyone shares. For example, toothpaste ads don't waste time telling you they will clean your teeth (point of parity). Instead, they highlight the toothpaste's whitening effects, or its tartar control ability, or its enamel strengthening capability (all points of differentiation, as not every toothpaste has all of those qualities).

My students at Duke will often spend precious time describing to campus employers why they picked Duke, but this is a mere point of parity, since all of the *other* people they are competing with are Duke students as well! Everyone's on equal footing here, so there's no point in spending time talking about how *equal* you are to your competition.

Points of differentiation are what make a product unique. Instead of having the same three Reasons that every other candidate is going to have, a point of differentiation approach would be to pick three Reasons in which you are at the very top of the candidate pool. Then, instead of expending effort trying to say something novel about the exact same qualities every other candidate is writing about, you'd instead devote your time and effort toward explaining how the employer will benefit from having that exceptional attribute of yours inside their organization.

So it's really up to you. You can pick Reasons you think the employer wants to hear or Reasons that genuinely reflect your biggest strengths. The former approach will be more traditional, but the latter approach will be more fun and likely give you a product you are happier with.

Can I have more (or fewer) than three RAC paragraphs?

Yes, you can state any number of Reasons why a company should consider you. However, nobody will ever criticize you for having three. (It also leverages a communications technique called the Rule of Three, which we'll discuss more in the next chapter.)

Furthermore, you can write cover letters that don't use RAC at all. In practice, though, I find those take far longer to write than a solid RAC Letter, and they tend to be *much* wordier, increasing the risk of typos and decreasing a hiring manager's willingness to take the time to genuinely read it. I don't really have any standard guidance for how to construct such novelty-style cover letters—besides "I'll know a good one when I see it," which isn't very helpful. I'm far more interested in giving you *one* efficient recipe that predictably works every time. RAC Letters remove all the ambiguity you might feel about what to say, where to say it, and in how many words.

Isn't that a bit impersonal and formulaic?

RAC is definitely formulaic, but not impersonal. In fact, because it's a formula, it allows you to focus on personalization rather than word count or format—almost like a job search–related Mad Lib.

This helps you convey your rationale directly and authentically, minimizing the need to include buzzwords and jargon. When every sentence both serves a specific purpose and moves your story forward, the temptation to embellish falls away.

Think you're funny? Prove it.

Let's say you lost a bet and you had to make one of your Reasons on your next cover letter your sense of humor. What's the best Anecdote you could present to convince this organization that it's true or important? (Simply saying "Everyone thinks I'm funny" won't cut it.)

A simple example of the "Reason is *true*" variety of Anecdote would be to pick one specific person who has actually told you that you are funny, such as "My nephew told me he thinks I'm the funniest person in the universe."

Or maybe you have other forms of proof such as accolades or awards: "I won the comic relief role of Donkey in our high school's production of *Shrek*" or "A joke I made in response to a Chrissy Teigen tweet once got over 500 likes, including one from Chrissy herself."

Alternatively, an example of the "Reason is *important*" variety of Anecdote would be citing information you learned in an informational meeting, like "Your company's head of design, Taylor North, mentioned how critical a sense of humor is when working late into the night to assemble client pitches on a tight deadline."

And that brings us to our Connection. How could an employer benefit from bringing your sense of humor into the organization?

Here are some ideas I had:

- My sense of humor would allow me to disarm client teams' potential apprehension at working with an outside consultant to gain their buy-in for our initiatives.

- My sense of humor would help me quickly form rapport with my cross-functional teammates, thereby allowing us to communicate more effectively and produce better products.

- My sense of humor could help me keep my teams energized and focused during long pitch sessions.

Again, RAC is less about having the right Reason and far more about Connecting it back to why the employer might benefit, demonstrating to them that you understand the role you are seeking, authentically wish to work in that role, and seek a good *mutual* fit.

Can you provide an example?

Sure. The body of the following example is just 220 words and contains three full RACs.

Dear Franklin,

I am interested in Darlington's open Marketing Associate position. After speaking with current associates Angela Charles and Nicole Yazzie, I believe I can contribute the following to your organization.

Problem Solving: I received two promotions in three years—the fastest rate possible at BiffCo—for my ability to break complex equipment issues into solvable tasks. My ability in this area would help me keep complex projects such as product redesigns and packaging changes running smoothly and on time at Darlington.

Analytics: While at BiffCo, I reduced part costs 30 percent by analyzing more than 12,000 unique inventory items to phase out obsolete parts, identify cheaper substitutes, and renegotiate contracts on our most heavily purchased items. This ability to use large amounts of data in creative ways would help me identify new markets and customer segments for Darlington's products.

Leadership: Nicole stressed to me how much Darlington values leadership in the form of firm-building. I have always strived to leave my mark on my organizations, both as Technology Officer in my graduate school's student government and as Excel Training Lead for BiffCo's new analysts. At Darlington, I would continue seeking leadership opportunities to strengthen the firm and build my internal network.

In closing, I think this would be a great mutual fit. Please contact me at 555-555-5555 or email@email.com at your earliest convenience.

Best regards,
Aditya

Don't I need to talk more about my accomplishments?

In almost *all* cases, a cover letter is accompanied by your resume. *That* is where your accomplishments are listed. If you use your cover letter to restate your resume, you are missing an opportunity.

Use your cover letter to tell readers what your resume *means to them.* Interpret it for them, as you would your findings from a project in an email to your boss's boss. Tell them what conclusions you suggest they draw based on the data provided, rather than just introducing them to the data without providing any additional analysis or perspective.

So what about facilitated cover letters?

These are both what you should be aiming for and much simpler than the unfacilitated version. They respond to an advocate's invitation: "Send me your resume and a cover letter that I can forward along to HR."

Whereas you would usually deliver an unfacilitated cover letter as a Word document or PDF, a facilitated cover letter can consist of a brief self-contained email (with resume attached) that your advocate can forward to HR with minimal additional commentary (read: effort). Thus it behooves you to keep it short and inoffensive. You've done the hard work of getting this person's cooperation, so allow their advocacy to do most of the talking, meaning you will keep this solicited cover letter much shorter than its unsolicited counterpart.

Can you provide an example of this as well?

Absolutely. You will see this is much less of a sales document and much more of an email that can be forwarded without additional context.

> Mariela,
>
> Thank you for your insights during our conversation earlier this week—it was both informative and motivating. On further reflection, I would indeed like to be considered for the open Marketing Associate position at Darlington.
>
> Per your request, I am attaching my resume. Do you need anything else from me at this time? Please let me know if you have additional questions, and I look forward to discussing our next steps.
>
> Best regards,
> Aditya

These truly are so short that I don't even have an official framework for them.

I'm totally kidding—here's the framework:

1. Acknowledge your advocate's request for your resume.
2. Reiterate your interest in the specific role you would like to be considered for.
3. Ask if they need additional information to keep the process moving forward.

As with resumes, it is critical your cover letters are error-free.

If your advocate spots a typo in your cover letter, they will not feel comfortable forwarding it to their colleagues, given that your work would be a reflection of their own judgment. Your gaffe would damage their peers' *perception of them*, so you might lose your advocate's willingness to fight for you.

How to avoid this? Don't send a cover letter as soon as you finish it. At that point, your eyes are numb to it. Get a good night's sleep before doing a final proof or, better still, share it with a loved one or use the grammar-checking software provided by your word processor or a third-party program such as Grammarly to ensure there are no mistakes. A typo or a wrong name can undo hours of effort that was about to yield results, and we don't want that!

Isn't there any more to this?

Honestly, no! Cover letters get easier once you realize each sentence serves a unique purpose and 200 words in length is totally fine! So let's wrap it up here:

TROUBLESHOOTING

What if I'm told by a possible advocate to submit a cover letter and resume online (rather than through them)?

It's impossible to know the specific hiring process at every firm in advance, since each employer has its own process. Thus, this sort of guidance may reflect one of a couple of scenarios.

First, this person is not truly an advocate and just wants to flush you into the online job posting black hole. This is unfortunate but commonplace. You still can and should mention this person's name in your cover letter. (Don't ask for permission, as they might not respond, leaving you in a bind.)

Second, it may be that you must apply online before they can advocate for you. In these situations, a true advocate (whom I call a "Booster" in *2HJS*) will often be apologetic about making you do so and clarify that that effort is necessary before they can proceed on your behalf.

PART 2

During the Interview

CHAPTER 5

The Big Four

What are the Big Four?

They are the four interview questions you are most likely to get at the start of your interviews, namely:

1. Tell me about yourself (TMAY).
2. Why this job?
3. Why our organization?
4. Why this sector/industry?

OK, so why do these questions need a nickname?

They need a nickname because of their sheer predictability and the fact that 60 percent[1] of interview decisions are made by the time an interviewer has asked them, according to a 2015 study of 691 interviews by Frieder, Van Iddekinge, and Raymark.

So, 5 percent of interviewers will make decisions on candidates within the first minute, based on their first impression. This may include situations where an interviewee is not appropriately dressed, has a weak handshake, smiles too much (or not enough), and similar turn-offs. I'm not endorsing such a superficial interviewing approach, but the data does show that one in twenty interviewers have decided before any questions are formally asked.

Another 25 percent make up their mind between the first and fifth minute, the period when small talk is usually covered, perhaps with a transition to TMAY. Again, just a statement of fact: *three in ten* interviews are decided based only on first impressions, small talk, and (possibly) TMAY.

An additional 30 percent make up their minds between the fifth and fifteenth minute. This is typically the time when the Big Four get asked. Thus, *60 percent* of interviews are decided based only on first impressions, small talk, and the Big Four. Over half of all interviews are decided based only on what I will cover in just this chapter, so you need to absolutely have your answers to these questions on lock.

Let's break down this study's results a bit further:

INTERVIEW TIME ELAPSED (MIN)	PERCENT OF INTERVIEWS DECIDED	CUMULATIVE PERCENTAGE DECIDED
0 to 1	4.9%	4.9%
1 to 5	25.5%	30%
5 to 15	29.5%	60%
Over 15	17.7%	78%
Post-interview	22.5%	100%

That can't be right. What about all those *other* interview questions I've been told to prepare for?

They are important, too, but *far less important* than getting the Big Four right.

You can see from the preceding table that 17.7 percent of interviews are decided during the remainder of the interview, which is typically when questions starting with "Tell me about a time when you . . ." and "What questions do you have for me?" will occur (we'll cover these in chapter 6). Thus, if you want to worry about *anything* in an interview, worry about the questions you know with near certainty will be asked during the portion of the interview when most decisions are made.

Preparing for the Big Four is the interviewing equivalent of learning to tie your shoes—you know it's going to come up again and again in life, so you might as well get good at it sooner rather than later.

The good news is: as interviewees, we actually *like* the Big Four.

Why do we like the Big Four?

First, as we already discussed, they are predictable; we'd rather know our interview questions in advance than not. Second, we know (thanks to the frameworks we will discuss in this chapter) that we will have excellent answers prepared for them. Third, for every one of the Big Four that *does* get asked, the interviewer is left with less time to ask us far more difficult questions such as "What is your biggest weakness?" and "Tell me about a time when you faced an ethical dilemma" (which we'll discuss in chapter 6 as well).

Now, not all of the Big Four are *always* asked but of the four, TMAY—or its equivalent, "Walk me through your resume" (see sidebar)—is the most pervasive, kicking off nearly all interviews once lead-in small talk is completed.

What about "walk me through your resume" (WMTYR)?

Although TMAY and WMTYR appear to be different questions, both seek the same information: namely, why and how does your journey into this interview make sense. Thus, we will answer both versions in the same manner, using a technique called FIT, which you'll learn more about later in this chapter.

Wait, not so fast! How do I navigate that small talk before TMAY?

Fair question! Let's back up a bit. The average interview will consist of the following phases, each with its own unique purpose in the interview:

PHASE #	PHASE	FOR INTERVIEWER, ANSWERS "DOES THIS CANDIDATE . . .
1	Small talk	. . . make a good first impression?"
2	"Tell me about yourself."	. . . have a story that makes sense?"
3	"Why this job, organization . . . ?"	. . . really want this (that is, do they know what they're getting and what we care about)?"
4	Behavioral interview questions	. . . have the necessary skills, mettle, and track record?"
5	Case interview questions (if applicable)	. . . have the necessary technical proficiency?"
6	"What questions do you have for me?"	. . . arrive prepared and use others' time wisely?"

This chapter will cover phases 1 to 3, specifically; the next two chapters will cover phases 4 and 6.

(Note about phase 5: If you know your interviews will feature a case interview component, in which interviewers ask you in-depth questions about how to solve problems you may encounter in the specific job you are hoping to acquire, I recommend seeking out an industry-specific case interviewing book for answering *those* questions. However, this book will still be crucial for helping you answer the other questions that do occur with high probability even in case-heavy interviews.)

Regardless of whether your interview features cases or not, it will always feature at least a minute or so of small talk, as first impressions are made, introductions are exchanged, seats are taken (if an in-person interview), initial rapport is established, and so on. No matter your feelings about small talk, it is critical that you take it seriously and do it well given our disposition toward confirmation bias.

What is confirmation bias?

Confirmation bias is humanity's tendency to arrive at quick first impressions about various people and subjects and then only pay attention to evidence that reinforces our first impressions while ignoring information that contradicts those impressions.

This traces back to our prehistoric days where our literal survival hinged upon quickly identifying whether an unfamiliar person or beast was a friend or foe. Those who waffled or chose poorly didn't get invited to future caveman parties.

Although we're no longer battling woolly mammoths or neighboring communities on the regular, we haven't lost that tendency to size up others astonishingly quickly (as evidenced by the 4.9 percent of interviews we learned about earlier that are decided in the first minute)! Furthermore, we all like to believe we are correct with the first impressions we make. It is uncomfortable to admit fault and fallibility where our judgments of others are concerned, so we avoid doing so whenever possible.

Confirmation bias isn't inherently *bad* for an interviewee, however—we just need to make sure it is working for rather than against us, meaning if we make a good initial first impression, our interviewer may overlook any verbal flubs, lack of clarity, or so-so stories we roll out from that point forward. The flip side is where we run into trouble. If we are awkward or off-putting during small talk, our interviewer is anchored with a *negative* first impression of us, and that will require a lot of work to overcome, if that's even possible.

So, best to get off to a good start.

So how do I get off to a good start in small talk?

For some of you readers, small talk comes naturally. If that is you, just keep doing you. However, it's never been intuitive to me; I've had to learn how.

In *2HJS*, I lay out my formula for small talk preceding *informational* interviews. Those are a bit different from job interviews, because in informationals, you as the job seeker manage the agenda. By contrast, in job interviews, the interviewer typically manages the agenda, which means they will try to establish rapport with you, rather than the other way around.

In other words, they lead and you follow.

Often, they will greet you and (if the interview is by phone or video rather than in-person) confirm if this time still works conveniently for you, which of course it should. Then they are likely to ask you a temperature-check question like "How is your day going so far?"—my personal favorite of all temperature-check questions.

What is a temperature-check question?

Temperature-check questions let the asker know if your small-talk partner is going to make this easy on you or not, just as checking the center of a baked potato informs you how much you'll want to eat it in its present state. A conversation partner makes this easy for you (or you for them) by giving them information to work with. Thus, "Fine. And you?" is not a good answer, because it gives your partner no new information to work with to establish rapport.

A better answer will provide a bit of personal information to which the conversation partner can react, such as "The sun is shining outside, so it's hard not to be happy on a day like today" or "I'm on my second cup of coffee, so it's going better now" or "I don't often make it to this part of downtown, but it's really charming!"

Skilled conversationalists will know to seize those bits of extraneous information to build rapport by asking informed follow-up questions, like "Are you more of a morning person than a night person?" or "How do you take your coffee? My parents always took theirs black, and now that's the only way I can drink it" or "Where in the city do you live? How does it compare?"

If whoever initiated the greeting for your interview doesn't immediately transition to a temperature-check question, I recommend asking one yourself to attempt to establish some rapport. (Note: Often they will use content from the Additional Information section of your CV to do this, so do not shy away from mentioning hobbies or interests there—after your objective biographical information, this is the section of your resume that gets the most attention!)

If, however, they ask you first—or they answer with a terrible "Fine. And you?" after you ask them—then *you* should provide a bit of extraneous information for your interviewer to work with to help establish rapport with *them*. They already have a job, so they don't have the same incentive to establish good chemistry that you do!

Once you know to listen for that piece of extraneous information during pre-interview small talk, it will become blindingly obvious when it's being offered to you. All you need to do is acknowledge it and respond to it. (This is a technique called "Yes, and . . ." in improvisational comedy. You are partners in small talk, so you should be prepared to work with whatever they give you and "yes, and" your way into a more meaningful interaction.)

In short, recognize that successful pre-interview small talk is more about listening than about speaking. When you build on comments your interviewer makes, you demonstrate that you are listening and that you find what they are saying to be of value.

If this feels unusually difficult or intimidating, don't feel badly; you simply haven't been trained for it. While many of us have taken speech classes at some point in our education or careers, woefully few of us have taken *listening* classes. So don't feel self-conscious if this all feels uncomfortable or counterintuitive at first—you will improve quickly!

OK, so we survived small talk. So TMAY is up next?

Yes, with near certainty.

I've answered this question hundreds of times before with zero complaints, do we really need to think about this one?

TMAY is an easy (and, dare I say, *fun*?) question to answer in casual settings when stakes are low. However, it's an easy question to answer *poorly* in an interview setting, and we need to crush this one. Remember, TMAY is the single interview question most likely to be asked in those first fifteen minutes of an interview when 60 percent of interview decisions are made. We can't leave such an important, influential question to chance.

And just because we've done something many times before in our lives doesn't mean we're good at it! Take folding a fitted bed sheet, for example—I've done this hundreds of times in my life, but the sheet still looks like a murdered prune when I finally give up and toss it into my closet.

Unfortunately, not only are the stakes higher when TMAY is asked in an interview than in your personal life, but also in interviews you are *definitely* being critically judged. Just because an answer feels good doesn't mean it's effective. Improvising your answer on the spot would certainly be natural, which is definitely a desirable quality, but it also is likely to lack structure, clarity, and impact.

Furthermore, spontaneity is just too casual for the circumstances. Your interviewer will appreciate the subtle deference you show when you've given this answer some thought in advance rather than just going where the moment takes you.

There are three *bad* ways to answer this question: (1) The Improv, (2) The Sales Pitch, and (3) The Transcript. We just covered why The Improv is a bad idea—it's too casual and random for the circumstances—so let's tackle The Sales Pitch next.

But this is an interview, right? Aren't I supposed to sell myself?

Yes, but not *yet*.

Think about what's happening in the interview when TMAY is asked. Usually you will have just engaged your interviewer in several minutes of small talk: you ask how their day is going, they ask you about your hobbies or cities you've lived in previously, and then they signal they are ready to start the formal Q&A portion of the interview by saying, "Well, I guess we should get started. Why don't you tell me about yourself?"

If you suddenly transform from the person who enjoys surfing, defends Cleveland's sports teams to the end, and tries to regularly visit family back home in Minnesota, into a robot rotely reciting "Here are the three reasons you should hire me," it is *very* jarring. Usually, such a sudden, inauthentic turn will leave your interviewer wishing for the quick return of the genuinely engaged interviewee they were speaking to mere moments before.

TMAY is a completely unique question. Consider it a fork, where every other interview question is a spoon. We need to use it for what it is good for (rapport-building), not what it is bad for (sales). More granularly, TMAY transitions you from small talk *into* sales, and you want to do this smoothly. Our guard goes up when we sense a sales pitch, but success in interviewing means systematically bringing your interviewer's guard *down*. So, no sales pitches. Not yet, at least.

Instead, imagine you are meeting a long-lost uncle or aunt for the first time. You would likely be warm toward them and tell them the honest truth about your life to date, since they are family, but you would also be slightly deferential, as they are your elder. That is the sort of energy and subtle formality I want you to bring to this answer.

However, no matter what you do, do *not* resort to The Transcript; that is worse than both The Improv and The Sales Pitch combined.

Why is The Transcript the worst?

At least The Improv and The Sales Pitch have *a* redeeming quality apiece: The Improv features (albeit overly) natural delivery, while The Sales Pitch focuses on the customer (your interviewer), telling them how they might benefit from bringing you into their organization. The Transcript has no redeeming qualities, yet job seekers routinely devote far too many hours to "perfecting" it.

The Transcript approach is what job seekers deliver when they know they need to prepare an answer to TMAY in advance but aren't comfortable delivering The Sales Pitch, so they mentally convert "Tell me about yourself" into its evil twin, "Walk me through your resume," and answer in the driest manner possible, reciting their schools attended, employers worked for, job titles earned, and responsibilities held, *all* of which are already in their resume.

Thus, unless your interviewer started the interview without looking at your CV at all (not likely, but possible), you are about to waste several minutes of both your lives by essentially reciting your resume out loud at them as if you were reading from a transcript—hence the name.

In practice, The Transcript typically sounds something like this:

> *I studied biology at the University of Illinois. After that, I took a job with MediFast as a regional sales representative for their pharmaceutical division. In this role, I was responsible for educating doctors about our product offerings, managing orders, and developing new clients, increasing sales in my region by 6 percent year-over-year. Next, I switched to CleanMed, where I moved to the project management side, helping the company bring new drugs to market . . .*

Literally, *every single thing* from this answer is already in that person's resume! No new content was shared, which is a poor use of everyone's time. Plus, everything interesting was skipped! *Why* did the job seeker change from Medifast to CleanMed? *Why* did the job seeker change from sales into project management? Transcript-style answers tend to focus on *what* the job seeker did, and interviewers would much rather hear *why* job seekers did what they did.

Interviewers just want to know that your overall story makes sense. They genuinely want to get to know who you are at the core—what motivates you and your decisions, why this organization and role make sense at this point in your life, and so on. If you deliver an answer that casts you as a mere passenger in your own life, that *doesn't answer their question. Don't do this!* They asked you to tell them about *yourself*—not your companies, job titles, and responsibilities—so you need to honor that request.

Finally, it's next to impossible to bring any sort of authentic energy to The Transcript, since job seekers are spending so much time trying to recall from memory what they are "supposed" to say that they have little brainpower left for sharing that information well. Thus, both content and delivery tend to be pretty awful.

That's why you need a framework that is loose enough to allow for a natural and authentic answer but structured enough to ensure that you deliver the information interviewers are seeking in a likable way; that's where the FIT Model comes in.

FIT (Favorite part-Insight gained-Transition made) will help you maintain all the goodwill and rapport you developed during the small talk and quickly catch them up on how you ended up here with them in this moment.

Isn't that an overly dramatic perspective to take on an interview question?

"Dramatic" is actually a *perfect* way to describe the FIT Model, not because it turns your life into a soap opera, but because it was developed from principles developed for drama—specifically, screenwriting.

Some years ago, I saw a video of Trey Parker and Matt Stone, creators of the long-running Comedy Central hit TV show *South Park*, speaking to a film class at NYU. (I've provided a link to this clip in the Resources section of my website, 2HourJobSearch.com.) In it, they described their approach to creating storylines.

Essentially, they said that when the elements of a story they're creating (what they refer to as "beats") are connected by "and then," they know their story is pretty bad. At that point, it's just a collection of detached facts without a logical structure connecting them.

They learned their stories flowed better when beats were connected by "but" or "therefore," as in: "Cartman is on his way to buy lunch *but* decides to spend his lunch money on comic books instead. *Therefore*, a hungry and penniless Cartman asks Kyle if he can borrow some money for lunch, *but* Kyle says that Cartman must first earn that money by carrying his backpack to school. *Therefore*, lazy Cartman cuts a hole in the backpack so that it can no longer hold heavy books, *but* this infuriates Kyle; *therefore*, Kyle . . ." and so on.

It makes sense, right? One element leads logically into the next, so the viewer is left with a satisfying, memorable story whose characters act logically based on who we've learned they are up to that point. This video clip remains a mainstay whenever I teach students in my class how to answer TMAY.

But what does this clip have to do with answering TMAY?

When people use The Transcript technique for answering TMAY, the beats of their answer are invariably connected by "and then"—"I did this, and then I did that, and then I did this other thing." Lots of activity, but no logic. Job changes just . . . happen. (Note: Starting a sentence with "Next, I . . ." and "After that, I . . ." is the TMAY equivalent of "and then," so don't do it!)

How can FIT help with this?

FIT connects the various stages of our career with "but" and "therefore." For each stage of your career to date (whether you have professional experience already or not), cite a Favorite part of that job or life stage. But if that job or life stage was perfect, you would have stayed forever, so at some point you had an Insight (your "but") that led you to make a Transition (your "therefore," although "thus" and "so" work nicely here as well), and you repeat for your next stage, and the next, and so on.

It will end up looking something like this (revisiting our example from earlier):

My **FAVORITE** part of studying biology while at the University of Illinois was breaking complex systems into their smaller components to understand how they worked at a granular level. My biggest **INSIGHT** from this experience was that I wanted to use my talent for understanding and explaining complex topics in a more applied setting. Therefore, upon graduation I **TRANSITION**ed into a role as a regional sales representative for MedFast's pharmaceuticals division.

My **FAVORITE** part of pharmaceutical sales was learning how to ask doctors the right questions to get them to share both their spoken and unspoken needs with me. However, I learned from the experience that I especially enjoyed the project management aspects of my work **[INSIGHT]**. There was unfortunately no path

for sales personnel to move into project management at MedFast,
so I decided to join CleanMed [TRANSITION] in order to facilitate
that career switch . . .

Won't our interviewers catch on to this pattern?

Maybe, but interviewers don't automatically hate frameworks. In fact, at times they will even *prefer* frameworks if they help convey critical information in an easy-to-understand fashion.

For example, in the next chapter we'll discuss the CAR Framework in depth. (If that rings a bell, it's because I mentioned CAR briefly back in chapter 2 in the context of the CAR Matrix.) If you don't use CAR (or one of its several variants), interviewers will actively *dislike* your answers, since they have to work harder to understand the information you're trying to convey. So even if you use a repetitive framework, it isn't automatically inauthentic or unlikable. It's more a matter of how you use it.

If you use frameworks to deliver relevant information concisely and acclimate your interviewer to a rhythm, in much the same way that pop songs acclimate us by repeating a chorus so that the song quickly seems familiar, it will work regardless of whether or not they recognize it as a pattern.

There is no trick here; interviewers are uninterested in performative novelty or innovation when they ask you interview questions! They simply want relevant information quickly.

How quickly?

Two minutes. Always. For every question. Two-minute answers are the industry standard, so sticking to this answer length helps you avoid unnecessary risk. A shorter or longer answer itself will never delight an interviewer, but it will alienate some of them; a one-minute answer will strike many as underbaked and not fully prepared, while a three-minute answer will strike many others as self-indulgent or similarly unprepared. There's no winning there, so don't take that chance.

Two-minute answers are the Goldilocks' porridge of interviewing—neither too hot (long) nor too cold (short), but just right.

I'm not actually comfortable saying something is my favorite. Can I use a different word?

What would you use instead?

Perhaps "really enjoyed" or "passionate about"?

You could, but you'd lose a lot of value in the process.

Why would I lose value?

You want to be authentic in your interview answers, correct? Then you will 100 percent need to be telling the truth if you use words like "really enjoyed" and "passionate," since they are both *much* harder to authentically convey than the relatively safe "favorite."

I realize it's counterintuitive—that disclosing something as personal as your favorite task at work could be less risky than saying you just really enjoyed an activity. However, when you say you really enjoyed an activity (or that you have passion for it, an even more drastic claim), your voice, body language, and affect need to match your words to keep your interviewer's trust.

Too often I see job seekers say they are passionate about things *they clearly are not passionate about*. Your interviewer will know something is off, and their skepticism will taint the rest of your interview.

Think about it this way—these are two statements about my feelings toward a particular household chore:

- My favorite household chore is cleaning the toilet.
- I really enjoy cleaning the toilet.

The first is true; the second is false. I don't *enjoy* cleaning the toilet, but cleaning the toilet is the chore I dislike the least (minimal effort, maximum impact!), making it my "favorite" chore by default.

If I say the first statement, I don't need to deliver a lot of energy to convince you that it is true. Even if I said it with a very flat affect—meaning without a smile or twinkle in my eyes—it is still both true and believable. However, if I were to say the second bullet in an interview with a flat affect, it would not be credible. "Really, Steve? I don't sense that you *really enjoy* cleaning the toilet." In other words, I'd have to bring a lot of verbal and nonverbal energy to credibly deliver the second statement to my interviewer.

More problematically, though, with the second statement I'd be lying. Don't lie in interviews!

I'm still just not comfortable using the word "favorite" over and over.

OK, I'll give you three more reasons to embrace "favorite" over the alternatives.

First, it makes you more interesting.

By definition, you can have only one favorite, so it removes the temptation to laundry-list responsibilities or projects you worked on and forces you to pick a side. And truly, say what was your genuine favorite part of the job! If you were an investment banker and your favorite part of that role was the scads of money you earned, own it!

Wouldn't that seem shallow?

Perhaps, but better to be shallow than dishonest. And it's perfectly OK to enjoy creature comforts sometimes! Especially when it was just a phase in your life.

That said, you still have to word it professionally and sensitively. You can't say, "My favorite part of investment banking was the MAD CAAAASH!" but you can certainly say, "My favorite part of investment banking, honestly, was the financial security it afforded me and my family. However . . ." and then you can pivot to the insight you gained (or the improvement you desired, such as having a greater quality of life) that led you in a different direction.

The nice thing about such radical candor is that your interviewer knows they can trust you after an answer like that. Everyone can relate to doing what you need to do to provide for your loved ones, so it's better to authentically defend the truth in a sensitive and professional manner than try to sell a lie that you think will sound better. Interviewers aren't looking to "identify the themes of your candidacy" during TMAY; they are just trying to get the bigger picture of who you are and what motivates you.

So, pick one and only one Favorite per role, and above all else, be honest.

What's your second reason?

"Favorite" is the ideal humblebrag.

There's an unusual semantic power in calling something your "favorite." You're clearly not bragging, but since you can have only one favorite by definition, employers tend to assume you're pretty good at it in a way they wouldn't have if you had said you "really enjoyed" or were "passionate about" it instead. Of all the elements of the job you could have named, you named *that one*, so interviewers will logically assume you are adept in that area. What candidate would call something they're bad or average at their favorite element of the job?

Now, some of your Favorites (as in the money example) may not actually be humblebrags. That's totally fine! It just makes the ones that *are* more credible, and it further puts your interviewer at ease that you're not running them through a sales pitch; you're just sharing with them your own personal truths.

I'm getting there, but give me your third reason.

OK, fine. The third reason to embrace "favorite" is because it's one less thing for you to remember when you head into an interview.

Are you saying I don't need to memorize or plan my Favorites in advance of an interview?

That's *exactly* what I'm saying. Feel free to prepare your Favorites in advance, but I also support you if you want to just say whatever's true to you in that moment—you lived it, so there's no memorization required. The authenticity matters more than the specific claim.

For example, if you were to ask me what my favorite part of working for the career center at Duke's business school is, on some days it would be the autonomy I'm granted to work on what I think will have the greatest impact. On other days, I would cite the intellectual freedom it grants me to try doing things in new ways. On still other days, I would say it's the incredible colleagues I have the privilege to work with every day. The reasons change from day to day, and I expect yours might as well.

Doesn't that leave a lot up to chance?

Again, this question is a fork and every other question is a spoon. It has a fundamentally different purpose: to establish rapport with your interviewer.

If you use it to try to score points, you will alienate your interviewer before you get to the part of the interview where you'll discuss your accomplishments in detail. So resist the temptation to sell yourself—just for this one question. You will reap great benefits from doing so, not just in terms of authenticity and likability, but also in memorability.

Memorability? How?

A 1969 study by Bower and Clark found that information delivered in a narrative fashion (meaning it was woven into a story) was between six and seven times more memorable than when delivered as a list.[2]

The Transcript answer to TMAY is essentially a list, as no logic connects the beats of your life. All whats, no whys. Thus, Transcript-style answers tend to be forgettable. If you've ever delivered The Transcript out loud, this will ring true, since you're usually half-asleep while delivering it. If even *you* don't find your answer interesting, your interviewer won't either.

FIT answers, in contrast, are stories. One beat logically leads into the next, so they are far more memorable. FIT also gives the interviewer information *worth remembering*. Specifically, new information that is flattering to you.

What if there wasn't an Insight that led me from one job to the next, like when I got promoted? Do I skip the Insight for that FIT?

Never skip Insight. You are never a victim of your own life's story; skipping Insight implies that you are.

Even when circumstances made some of your life choices seemingly inevitable, you could have just started running in one direction and never looked back. But most people don't do that. They survive. They fight. They keep going—if not for themselves, then for those who rely on them. You made decisions every step of the way.

Granted, sometimes running away and/or declining to change roles would have been a very bad idea—such as going AWOL to avoid a promotion in the military. In any case, you still chose to make the move up (or over, if it was a sideways promotion).

Promotions are something to be celebrated and highlighted, yet very often I see my job seekers completely ignore their own promotions—often while spending far too *much* time on job responsibilities or describing their previous organization's capabilities—when promotions are one of the only critical things to mention during your answer to TMAY! Promotions demonstrate that your organizations liked you enough to pay you more and give you more responsibility. How can that not be worth mentioning?

But that takes time! Don't I need to make sure my interviewer understands what my previous company did?

Do you, though?

The prompt is "Tell me about yourself." Does information about your previous employer help your interviewer get to know you?

I guess not, but how do I craft a FIT if I didn't feel I had any choice but to accept my promotion?

I recommend making your Insight something like "I was seeking to have more responsibility" or "manage a larger team" or "gain exposure to a new part of the business," and your Transition something like "so when I was offered a promotion, I happily accepted."

Stating that you had agency in your own life seems like a small detail, but it leaves a much more positive impression.

What if the reason I changed jobs was because I was laid off?

Then you are part of a worldwide community that understands where you're coming from! You still had an Insight about what sort of job to pursue next, even if it was a job you didn't particularly enjoy just to make ends meet. (The "I" in FIT originally stood for "Improvement desired" before it became the more general "Insight gained," so for layoffs, you may wish to switch it back to "Improvement desired," which was finding employment once again following a layoff that wasn't your choice.)

Some job seekers will feel comfortable not mentioning the layoff at all, choosing instead to focus that particular Insight on an aspect of that role they sought to improve, while others won't be able to avoid mentioning their layoff and feel they are delivering an authentic answer. The worst-case scenario would be to dance around any mention of your layoff, but your discomfort while avoiding the topic is still obvious to your interviewer. My advice is to avoid mention of it if it feels authentic to you, and if that does not feel authentic to you, address it directly as your Insight/Improvement in that particular FIT.

Well, what if I *hated* my job?

Then you are part of an even *more* worldwide community who understands where you're coming from. Just be honest.

Didn't see that coming, did you?

Authenticity is key in TMAY. Sometimes you get laid off. Sometimes a parent or child gets ill and you become a full-time caregiver. Even if you didn't choose to be downsized, you chose how to respond to downsizing, and that in turn informs your interviewer about the kind of candidate to whom they are speaking.

However, just because I recommend being honest about your setbacks does *not* mean I condone negativity. For every negative thing you can think to say, there's a positive way to reframe it.

Don't like your in-laws? "I wish we were closer."

Don't think your previous employer appreciated you? "I worked hard to get my work recognized."

Think it's too cloudy in the Midwest? "Living in the Midwest made me really appreciate sunny days."

Speaking of FIT statements, my Insight for my own life *could* mention that I found my brief stint as a chemical engineer tedious and repetitive, but my FIT statement would look something like this:

> My **FAVORITE** part of being a chemical engineer was gaining deep expertise in Microsoft Excel—if I could think it, I knew how to make Excel do it. However, I decided I wanted to apply that analytical rigor to a wider variety of challenges **[INSIGHT]**, so I moved into strategy consulting **[TRANSITION]**.

Make no mistake: I hated chemical engineering. However, that's my baggage, not my interviewer's, and professionals handle their own baggage.

Here's how we as job seekers handle our own baggage during TMAY: we find something positive to say about every experience, and we frame our Insights around things we wanted to do differently or more consistently rather than around what we disliked or were running away from.

The art of a good Insight statement with FIT is to say even negative things in a positive way. Once you form the habit, you'll be surprised how automatic this instinct becomes in both interview and non-interview settings.

Is there anything special to know about Transitions in FIT?

No, actually. You don't have anything to memorize, since you know what job you took next. Just ensure that the statement that leads into your Transition starts with a logical transitional word like "therefore," "thus," or something similar to make it easy for your listener to know that your Transition resulted directly from the Insight that you had.

So how do I start my FIT answer? Do I just dive in with my first Favorite?

No, you'll definitely want to provide a brief orienting sentence to help transition your interviewer into your first FIT.

I recommend starting wherever your own "hero's journey" began. For some it's their hometown. For others, it's their family circumstances. For others, it was what they studied in college. For still others, their current life path didn't really get under way until their first or second job, so choose whatever starting point (1) feels authentic to you, and (2) allows you to tell your story within two minutes.

Personally, I like starting with a hometown, because everyone has one and it humanizes you as an interview candidate. "I'm originally from Delhi, and I've always loved numbers" will quickly orient your interviewer, just as "I'm from Minneapolis, the youngest of four kids, but I wanted to expand my horizons beyond Minnesota, so upon graduation from high school I decided to join the US Navy" would, but skipping over a hometown with something like "My earliest passion was performance, and that led me to study theater at Berkeley" or "Both of my parents were doctors, so that led to my early interest in health care" is fine too.

The FIT structure doesn't have to be rigidly observed for 100 percent of your answer, but it will help you progress through the "meat" of your answer. The key element of a good orienting sentence is simply that it is concise and that *it doesn't sell*. It's OK to share a personal motivator (as in the examples earlier with "performance" and "numbers"), but remember that the purpose is to impart key background on you rather than to "establish themes" or impress your interviewer. FIT works well because it is honest, and nothing sabotages an honest FIT answer more than a sales-y opening statement like "Before I begin, there are three themes I want to call your attention to in my career: my analytical skills, strong work ethic, and leadership ability."

The key is to keep these *short*. FIT works so well because it tells a story rather than a detached series of facts to make your personal information more memorable, so we want to get into the buts and therefores as quickly as possible!

So do I end my FIT answer with my Favorite part of my current or most recent role?

I get this question a lot! My recommendation: stick the landing for an ideal finish by leading them into the "Why this role?" question.

My own FIT answer heading into business school to switch into marketing would have looked like this:

> My **FAVORITE** part of being a Senior Business Analyst was iden-
> tifying and designing workstreams that would provide the most
> impact to our clients, but I realized I wanted to have a "home
> team"—a single organization that I could follow over a longer
> period of time than what consulting allowed **[INSIGHT]**, given I
> was switching clients every couple of months. Thus, I decided to
> return to business school **[TRANSITION]** in order to pursue my MBA
> and switch into CPG [consumer packaged goods] marketing.

The end.

The nice thing about finishing your TMAY answer in this fashion (with a hint at the role you're seeking) is that it makes the transition from TMAY into "Why this role?" feel like a spontaneous conversation, improving your chemistry with your interviewer—even if that question was already the next one up on the interviewer's list, as it very often is. Even if it wasn't, though, your interviewer will often go ahead and ask you anyway, given that elegant segue, since it just *feels right*.

Bingo.

The key here is to *tease* your interest in the role you're interviewing for, but not speak at any length about it. If you speak about it for too long, the interviewer may feel it unnecessary to actually ask you why you want the role. But you *want* that question, and you want a full two minutes to answer that question. Remember, we like the Big Four because we know we have excellent answers ready for them and because they give our interviewer less time to ask tougher questions.

But what if the interviewer *doesn't* ask me "Why do you want this role?" They don't always ask!

Relax. If interviewers want to know something, they will ask. You might even say that's their one job.

The common mistake I see job seekers make here out of fear is trying to cram their responses to TMAY, "Why this role?," and "Why our organization?" into a single answer. Not only does this sell your answers to both of these questions very short, but it also spoils a few of the interviewer's future questions, so now *they* are forced to think harder to improvise what else they can ask (and, again, interviewers hate having to think harder during an interview). This just increases the odds that you get harder questions later in the interview, so resist this temptation.

Anecdotally, I would say that TMAY is asked in about 95 percent of interviews, and two "Why?" questions—most commonly "Why this job?" and "Why our organization?"—are asked in about 90 percent of interviews. So, far more often than not. Don't abbreviate your answer just to accommodate the one-in-ten interviews where it might not get asked.

So how do I answer these "Why?" questions?

Want some good news? You've already learned how!

In the previous chapter, we discussed how to create lean and mean cover letters using the RAC (Reason-Anecdote-Connection) Model. While we will occasionally use full RAC statements (or RACs) to answer "Why?" questions in interviews, the Connection won't always be necessary (or possible, due to the two-minute time limit we discussed), so in this chapter we'll just use the first two parts, Reason-Anecdote, as our default structure.

So how do I start my Reason-Anecdote answers to "Why?" questions?

Start by stating how many Reasons you have. This will put your interviewer at ease, so they know—based on how long describing your first Reason takes—that you will be done within two minutes.

How many Reasons should I have?

There's no set number! However, lists of three are often considered neither too long nor too short, making three the perfect amount of prepared Reasons ready for an interview answer. (There's even a Latin phrase for this concept, *omne trium perfectum*—roughly translated, "every set of three is complete." This is also often referred to as the Rule of Three.)

Think about how many popular phrases occur in threes! Everything from "Snap! Crackle! Pop!" to "Stop, drop, and roll" to "On your mark, get set, go." (Reread this book, and you'll notice a recurring theme of lists of three!) By contrast, how many popular phrases with *four* elements can you think of?

No interviewer will be upset with a list of three. An added benefit of a list of three is it helps you break up your answers into more memorable chunks, spending thirty to forty seconds on each one, and thirty to forty seconds happens to be exactly how much time it takes to get through a garden-variety Reason-Anecdote!

That said, if you truly have only one, two, or four reasons for one of the "Why?" Big Four questions, adjust your timing accordingly so you still finish in two minutes.

So what should my three Reasons be?

As with cover letters, there are no "right" answers. The heart wants what it wants. The best we can do is be honest and authentic about our motivations.

The best place to start—as with so many other tasks in life (and earlier in this book, for that matter)—is to make a list. Do a brain dump of every Reason you can think of why you want this job, this organization, and this sector or industry. Get them out of your head and onto paper; this makes it easier to evaluate your Reasons for using them in interviews. And as you keep adding to those lists over time, you'll identify even-better Reasons that were not immediately apparent to you.

What if one of the Reasons I want to work for an organization is the great people they hire? I've heard that that answer is pretty overused . . .

It is *definitely* overused, but that doesn't mean it can't be an excellent answer, if properly sourced and tied back to how the employer will benefit from making *you* one of their great people. *This* is exactly what Reason-Anecdotes are designed to do.

Here's what this "the great people you hire" Reason can look like when Aditya (the job seeker from our cover letter example in chapter 4) does *not* use the Reason-Anecdote format in his answer for Darlington Electronics:

> *There are three main reasons I want to work for you. The first is the great people who work there. Everyone I have met has just been so warm and friendly, and I know that not every corporate culture is like that. It's really important to me to work with great people, so I think your company would be a really good fit for me.*

Good energy, perhaps, but very little actual content.

Aditya just sort of states a Reason ("the great people"), restates it, adds in some global truths (like "not every organization has great people" or "not every interview answer has content"), and then finishes on a "why this is good for *me*" sentiment.

This sort of substance-free answer may not insult his interviewer, but it definitely won't impress them.

Furthermore, such an answer puts him at risk of being called out, as I was in one of my all-time favorite interviews. I was asked why I wanted to join a particular organization, and the first Reason I gave my interviewer was their collaborative culture. My interviewer immediately stopped me and said, "How do you know we have a collaborative culture?" Uh-oh.

In essence, he told me, "Prove it," and I was off script the entire rest of the interview, and it was a glorious learning experience. (And by that I mean "awful." Like I said, framing Insights positively becomes automatic after a while . . .)

So what distinguishes a good answer to a "Why?" question?

Above all else, "Why?" answers must be (1) *authentic*, (2) *specific* (to the employer, role, sector, or industry, depending on the question), and (3) *informed*, a delineation first proposed by my Fuqua colleague Shawn Pulscher (with an assist from his equally brilliant wife Maureen, who fortunately for our team is a corporate recruiter).

While Aditya's Darlington answer might have been *authentic*, it was neither *specific* nor *informed*. Aditya could have said those exact same words to any other employer. That is the single clearest sign of a terrible "Why?" answer.

How does Aditya know the company hires great people, for example? The easiest way around this would be for him to mention *specific* people he met who reinforced this impression or, better yet, told him that the organization's people are truly what differentiates them from their competitors in their space (making Aditya *informed*). In other words, reference the informational meeting in the form of an Anecdote. Without actual names, it just seems like Aditya is trying to bluff his way through his answer.

Yes, this means that the information you learn when doing informational meetings *does* actually prove useful later! In fact, the majority of the employer and industry research you conduct before your interview—whether online or in conversations with current employees—should be with the express purpose of answering "Why?" questions in an authentic, specific, and informed way.

So let's take a look at what Aditya's answer for Darlington Electronics could look like if he uses the Reason-Anecdote format:

There are three main reasons I want to work for Darlington.
*The first **REASON** is the great people. I've had the pleasure of*
chatting on Zoom with one of your VPs, Finley Richards, and
she said that she's worked for a lot of companies that have
called themselves a family, but Darlington is the first one that
*actually lives up to that claim [**ANECDOTE**]. That really left an*

impression on me, since I very carefully choose my communities based on their shared values, from employers to schools to book clubs to volunteer groups.

That is what we are striving for: *authentic, specific,* and *informed,* with every sentence adding unique value. Only in this second example does Aditya show that he knows what he's getting himself into at Darlington and what the Darlington community cares about, demonstrating thoughtfulness and purpose in his communication. In contrast, his answer in the first example just tosses word salad for thirty seconds, demonstrating neither understanding of the organization nor a sense for his fit within it.

In short, the key to using possibly overused answers is to *attribute* them, to either a current employee (as in our first example), a credible media publication, or other relevant research. If he's comfortable doing so and it matches his style, Aditya may also choose to tack on a Connection, turning his Reason-Anecdote answer into a traditional RAC, for an even more specific and informed answer, like so:

I think my genuine appreciation of both great people and great community will let me gain the trust of my work teams quickly and help me uphold Darlington's "Decency First" credo.

This is truly optional, however, and it may not be possible within your two-minute limit for all Reasons, so you should use it situationally.

In what situations should I add a Connection to my Reason-Anecdote?

I find adding a Connection to be most effective when your answer might be considered a bit trite or clichéd (as that "the great people" answer often can be when not using Reason-Anecdote or a full RAC) or when the benefit of your Reason to the employer is not immediately clear (if you're saying you are interested in working for this company because they are the market leader—what do they get out of that?).

Aditya makes very explicit in his Connection what the benefit of selecting *him* would be to Darlington's culture. By doing that extra step of logic for the interviewer rather than relying on them to connect the dots, Aditya becomes a much more easily liked candidate. Instead of having to think, his interviewer can just make a note: "Will gain trust of work teams faster" and "Gets our 'Decency First' credo" and keep listening.

Even if the interviewer disagrees that Aditya's appreciation for a family-like work culture will help him gain the trust of his work teams quickly, they will appreciate that he at least *tried* to translate his own interests into a benefit for Darlington as well, demonstrating deference to the true customer in the interview room.

Do Reason-Anecdote and RAC work the same way for "Why this role?" and "Why this sector?" as well?

Yes, they do. So let's finish out this chapter by giving you an annotated sample response to each of the other two "Why?" questions from the Big Four, using Aditya and Darlington as our examples. (Keep in mind that the Connection is optional and up to Aditya's discretion, but I'll include Connections for both examples as illustrations.)

Here is a possible answer if Aditya is asked "Why does the Marketing Associate role appeal to you?" during his Darlington interview:

*I think three reasons stand out in particular about this position. The first **REASON** is the role's emphasis on analytics. I noticed the job description described how one of the key responsibilities of the Marketing Associate role was to analyze Nielsen data to identify trends in Darlington product sales and identify opportunities for growth. As a civil engineer, I became very comfortable with manipulating data in both Microsoft Excel and Access and using that information to tell a compelling story about why a particular decision should be made **[ANECDOTE]**. I think my ability to craft stories out of data will help me identify developing trends in the home electronics market faster and communicate our products' benefits to consumers in an easy-to-understand way **[CONNECTION, optional]**.*

*The second **REASON** is . . .*

If asked "Why do you want to work in the consumer electronics sector?", here's how Aditya could use RAC in his answer again:

*I think three reasons in particular stand out for me. The first **REASON** is my lifelong passion for home electronics. I got the Darlington SuperPro 6200 gaming system for my birthday one year when I was in grade school [ANECDOTE]. That got me interested in electronics at a very young age. I started reading industry blogs, debating new platforms' merits with my friends, and even listening in on investor calls! I think my long history of following electronics trends and discussing products with fellow fanatics would help me effectively communicate with not only consumers who love Darlington products, but also the engineers who design them and the sales team who take them to market [CONNECTION, optional].*

*The second **REASON** is . . .*

Is that all there is to this?

Indeed. Just remember: *authentic, specific,* and *informed.*

And with that, we've made it through those critical initial fifteen minutes of our interviews. We'll deal with the remaining interview time in the next chapter, but great work so far! I realize it's a lot to take in, but there's only one formula we'll learn in the next chapter, so the hardest work is behind us.

Are your answers to Big Four questions consistently two minutes in length? ✓

Are the elements of your answer to TMAY separated by "but" and "therefore" rather than "and then"? ✓

Do you state one and only one Favorite aspect of each of your career stages during TMAY rather than laundry-listing responsibilities or tasks you performed? ✓

Are your answers to "Why?" questions *authentic, specific,* and *informed*? ✓

TROUBLESHOOTING

What if I worked only briefly for a series of start-ups and I can't get through FITs for each one within two minutes?

Feel free to combine similar experiences to conserve time. Instead of talking about each of three start-ups individually, you could say something like this:

"During my first two years out of undergraduate, I worked for a series of three different start-ups as a Java programmer. My favorite part about those roles was communicating with the product manager to identify ways to design the code with future enhancements in mind. However, I wanted to have more formal training than what the start-up environment provided, so I decided to join industry leader TechTitan as a programming team lead to access those training opportunities."

What if I've had a long career already? I can't possibly get through all of those FITs within two minutes!

Feel free to start later in your career. Typically, we do more impressive iterations of our work later in our careers, so simply

continued

skip the earlier, less-impressive versions of the work you are currently doing if that helps you more easily finish on time.

Would FIT work for elevator pitches, too?

Ah, the fabled elevator pitch. As a matter of fact, FIT *will* work for the elevator pitch, but let's talk about why I've relegated my entire discussion of elevator pitches to this FAQ.

Elevator pitches are a dated concept. The name refers to this hypothetical scenario from the mid-1900s or so where you'd find yourself by good fortune in the very same elevator as a higher-up in your organization, and you only have the length of that ride to convince them why you're the scrappy up-and-comer who deserves a chance at the corner office in the hopes that they like the cut of your jib.

Maybe it appeared in a movie once. No idea, but the "elevator pitch" concept has endured, despite what must have been an apparent insatiable global appetite for unsolicited sales pitches in enclosed spaces back in the day. Regardless, careers are no longer made or broken by chance encounters in elevators these days. The only time elevator pitches seem to be expected and not despised are during career fairs and conferences where employees of a company manage a booth and job seekers line up hoping to leave a great impression with them in the minute or two they are given.

What you want to do in this short period of time is to give this employee a story they can remember and get invested in, and FIT is a much better way to accomplish this than reciting a list of buzzwords and self-congratulations to an employee whose mind is definitely wandering to other things while you are talking.

My recommendation is to read the room. For how long are the job seekers preceding you speaking before the employer interjects (knowing that the first question they typically ask candidates is TMAY)? If it's two minutes (not unusual for one-on-one interactions), your full FIT TMAY answer will work. If it's just thirty seconds, I'd recommend shortening your answer to just your single most recent FIT, ending with the desired Transition that leads to your interest in this employer's booth at this moment. (Note that this short version, what I call a FIT Pitch, also works at networking events when one or more of a group of people are asked to introduce themselves.)

To me, this FIT Pitch is the modern evolution of the elevator pitch. Don't brag at strangers. Instead, give them a story they can invest in and possibly recall later despite the dozens of other sales-oriented elevator pitch monstrosities they'll hear that day.

Besides, what elevator rides are a full two minutes long anyway these days?

CHAPTER 6

Behavioral Interview Questions

What are behavioral interview questions?

With behavioral questions, the interviewer attempts to predict your future fit and performance by asking you to describe past instances when you've demonstrated certain abilities and qualities. This ensures that you have the necessary skills, mettle, and track record for the job (see the interview phases table on page 77 for a refresher). These questions almost always start with phrases like "Tell me about a time when you . . ." or "Give me an example of when you . . ."

Those phrases could end in hundreds of ways, though! How do you prepare for hundreds of possible questions you won't know in advance?

First off, don't panic! It's easier than you think.

You will identify finite, self-contained accomplishments and experiences from your past that demonstrate desirable qualities in an employee, and then you will build two-minute stories around each one. Realistically, you need to prepare only about a dozen.

How can a dozen stories answer hundreds of different possible questions?

Two ways: First, each story has the potential to answer *many* different possible questions, and second, there are only so many positive qualities, skills, and traits employers can ask you about.

We'll start by identifying the stories you are likely to tell. Then we'll match those stories to the attributes that interviewers are most likely to ask you about. Finally we'll create stories to fill in any potential gaps. Sound manageable?

Yes, but I reserve the right to change my mind later. So how do I identify the stories I'm likely to tell?

Your resume is a great place to start, *especially* if you created your bullet points using the accomplishment statement format we discussed back in chapter 2. (I told you that legwork would pay off later!)

Each bullet point is a story you could tell in an interview. In fact, I've had interviews that consisted *only* of interviewers asking me about bullet points that they found particularly interesting, so it's critical that each is its own story (complete with results), rather than a summary of responsibilities.

While we have this information written down in your resume, I recommend moving it over to Excel. Now is the time to start building your CAR (Challenge-Action-Result) Matrix.

What is a CAR Matrix?

The CAR Matrix is the spreadsheet you will use to ensure you have stories prepared for common skills or traits that employers may ask you for examples of in an interview. Then, when you receive a question investigating that skill or trait, you will know which CAR story to tell.

What is CAR again?

CAR stands for Challenge-Action-Result, the interviewing industry standard for answering behavioral interview questions.

There are variants of CAR employed by different career coaches—some call it PAR (for Problem-Action-Result) or STAR (for Situation-Task-Action-Result)—but all career coaches teach some variety of this basic structure. Furthermore, all interviewers have come to expect it—so much so that many will become frustrated if it's not used, since they then have to work a lot harder to figure out what a candidate is saying, instead of just being able to write down C, A, and R on their notepad and fill in the blanks! If you make your interviewer work harder to understand you than other candidates do, they are going to associate you with additional work, and that's not going to help your chances.

In essence, for any interview question that asks you to detail how you've faced a challenge or demonstrated a particular quality in the past, you provide the Challenge that you faced, the Actions *you* (not your team) took, and the Results that you and your team achieved.

So how do we turn our resume bullets into CAR stories?

In your resume, your bullet points (if you formatted them as accomplishment statements) followed the same structure, but you omitted the Challenge due to space constraints. Thus, each bullet point is a CAR story you could tell, which should give you almost a dozen CAR story topics to develop into interview-ready CAR stories without even doing any additional work.

To convert each bullet into a CAR story, you'll briefly summarize the Challenge you faced (and any extenuating factors that help you establish that accomplishment's level of difficulty), organize and elaborate on your Actions—especially those that enabled you to achieve the exceptional Results you cited in your resume—and identify any additional Results not already written in your resume.

You can easily create your own CAR Matrix, or you can download one from the Resources section of my website at 2HourJobSearch.com/Resources. It looks something like the following chart.

#	STORY	COMMUNICATION SKILLS	ANALYTICAL THINKING	TEAMWORK	LEADERSHIP	CREATIVITY
1	**Challenge:** Consumers weren't washing hands for long enough. I was not formally assigned the project, but found the challenge interesting and my request for time to work on it was approved.					
	Action: (1) Researched the problem. I learned the leading factors were lack of awareness and boredom with the task. **(2)** Created prototype soaps that signal to users when a hand wash is complete. **(3)** Identified early-adopter audiences in hospitals and elementary schools, then presented best prototype to management.		X		X	X
	Results: Received buy-in from management and the product was later patented.					
2	**Challenge:**					
	Action:					
	Results:					
3	...					

The CAR Matrix extends both to the right (with additional attributes you suspect employers may ask you about) and downward (with rows for as many stories as you will be prepared to discuss).

From this populated sample matrix, you can see that a single story can be used to answer multiple questions—an "X" marks the topics that a particular story can answer (in this case, questions about analytical thinking, leadership, and creativity).

You should start by loading all of the accomplishments you listed in your resume into the Story column in CAR format, and then mark with an "X" the skills or traits that each story showcases (or, if you wish, an "XX" if the story is *particularly* good at answering that prompt). Once done, you can identify any skills or traits for which you don't readily have any stories to cite from your CV—these gaps are potential interview liabilities, so you would then look more deeply into your work history, volunteer activities, or school experiences to find a suitable answer so you are prepared in case a question about that quality gets asked.

So how long will it take for me to talk through one of these CAR stories in an interview?

Two minutes. Always two minutes. Any more and you'll overstay your welcome. Any less and you will appear unprepared.

Occasionally, employers will interrupt you during your story to ask you clarifying questions—or just to push you off script. This is rare, but it does happen. In such cases, focus on deeply listening and understanding what your interviewer is trying to learn, asking clarifying questions as necessary (for example, "I just want to be certain I'm giving you the information you're seeking—are you asking for more information about . . . ?").

However, in the vast majority of cases when you are asked a behavioral interview question, you will be allowed (and expected) to speak for two minutes.

How do I divide up those two minutes?

You should spend about fifteen seconds on the Challenge you faced, ninety seconds on the Actions you took, and the remaining fifteen seconds on the Results you achieved.

How can I summarize my Challenge in just fifteen seconds?

Don't go into detail. It's really that simple.

However, just because the *concept* is simple doesn't mean the execution is. Embracing the "no details" perspective on Challenges can take some adjustment.

Quick poll: Do you prefer simple explanations or complex explanations?

I prefer simple explanations.

Good! So does literally everyone else, including your interviewer, so we're all on the same page.

With job seekers I train, the temptation is to go into *great* detail to set up their stories—sometimes they will describe the Challenge for a full ninety seconds before they even get to their first Action! That is the equivalent of giving your interviewer a complex explanation when they (again, like everyone else) would prefer a simple one.

Well, my background is very specific. How are interviewers going to understand my Actions if they don't understand the context?

You'll be surprised how effectively interviewers can fill in the gaps.

My favorite example of how effectively we as human beings can fill in narrative gaps is this famous six-word story (dubiously attributed to Ernest Hemingway):

"For sale: baby shoes; never worn."

In fact, there's a whole genre of writing, called "flash fiction," that demonstrates in 280 characters, fifty words, or some other length constraint how little context is necessary to tell a full story. So even if your projects were very technical, there is still a simpler way to describe them. Here are some measures you can take:

- **OMIT ANY DESCRIPTION OF WHAT THE COMPANY YOU WORKED FOR DID.** This isn't relevant to *your* CAR story, which is entirely about what *you* (not your team) did. If your prior organizations are not well known or well understood, add one line of italicized text under their name in your resume, describing what sort of work they did.

- **ELIMINATE ANY JARGON, ACRONYMS, OR TERMS THAT REQUIRE EXPLANATION.** Instead, go one level higher. For example, instead of "dunnage for remanufactured AMLOG-15 transmissions," say "plastic shipping containers."

- **LIMIT DESCRIPTIONS OF WHAT YOUR TEAM WAS ATTEMPTING TO DO.** The work *you* did is most relevant. For those career coaches who teach STAR (for Situation-Task-Action-Result) instead of CAR, the Situation describes what your team did, whereas the Task describes your specific piece of the project.

Challenge tends to be simpler for most job seekers to grasp than Situation-Task—that's why I prefer CAR.

In short, embrace the fact that any item you bought, sold, processed, created, tested, or studied can be described as a "widget" for CAR story purposes. The details of the widget don't matter; what matters is the actions you took to ensure that whatever needed to happen with that widget got done *well*.

Sample Challenge statements can be as simple as:

- "A piece of technical equipment I was responsible for stopped working properly, so I had to fix it as quickly as possible."
- "I was tasked with lowering my department's costs by 20 percent."
- "I had to bring my client back into compliance with industry regulations or they would be shut down."

Is there anything I need to mention in my Challenge statement?

Your Challenge statement should be short, but if there's one thing you *need* to be sure to mention, it's any context that helps convey why this was a particularly strong example of your abilities. Often, this involves complications. Here are some examples of contextualizing difficult Challenges to help establish their level of difficulty:

- "I had to design a component for our company that was unlike any other we'd ever produced before."
- "I needed to convince senior buyers at my client to adopt a new contract template, despite the fact that they were much older than I was, they were all men [if you yourself are not], and the new contract would likely reduce the kickback incentives they received from their vendors."
- "After a sudden departure at the executive level, I had to take over a team of twelve people on three continents and complete a critical project in half the normal amount of time."

So how do I transition into my Actions?

Remember how we discussed stating up front the number of Reasons you have for "Why?" questions? We're going to do that here as well. I recommend numbering them in your CAR Matrix so they are easy to count and remember. In general, I (again) recommend having three, plus or minus one.

If you had to take more than just three Actions to meet your Challenges and you are having difficulty narrowing them down for a two-minute CAR story, there are two approaches I recommend: the Cherry-Pick and the Ready-to-Eat. Feel free to pick your favorite.

What is the Cherry-Pick approach?

The Cherry-Pick involves selecting a few Actions from the ten or so you performed to complete your Challenge. Personally, I'd recommend skipping over the more mundane Actions and focusing on the ones that were most clever or disproportionately impacted your outcome.

Your CAR stories are essentially your "greatest hits," which are determined in part by the exceptional Results you achieved. Thus, help your interviewer understand that you did this project *better* than another employee would have in your shoes—this generally means highlighting above-and-beyond or special approaches you took that unlocked those exceptional Results. In short, you will cherry-pick only your best actions and highlight them here.

What if I did the same kind of project over and over, so that many of my CAR stories consist of that one type of project?

Remember to think smaller, as we did with our resumes. Sometimes CAR stories—just like our resume's bullet points—cover projects that lasted weeks or months; in other cases, a CAR story will have elapsed over the course of a single day (maybe even concurrently with one or more of your longer stories!).

That said, if you expect to reference a similar kind of project multiple times and that project requires many Actions—let's say ten—you should highlight three of them in one of your CAR stories and in the other highlight three *different* Actions. This ensures that your interviewer won't get bored and that you demonstrate a broader variety of skills than just highlighting the same Actions time and time again.

Can't I just list all of the ten Actions I performed? I can surely do that in ninety seconds.

Don't do that. Then it just becomes a laundry list of ten items, and we know by now that lists should be between two and four items long if you want your audience to remember anything you said.

Typically, when I see job seekers adopt this approach, it is very similar to the "and then" faux pas the *South Park* creators discussed: "I did this, and then I did this, and then I did this," bouncing around from tactic to tactic until a miracle occurred and the project got done. Any exceptional Result is undermined by the fact that the candidate didn't have time to explain why one or more of their Actions were exceptional. Even if the exceptional quality happens to be that they managed to take on so many Actions in such a short period, with such a long list there simply isn't time to explain that that was the case. As a result, it appears that the candidate just did what they were told and was fortunate enough to be hitched to a lucky star.

It's important to convey to your interviewer that either you had a plan—that one step led into the next—or you knew what was exceptional about your Actions so you can account for your exceptional Results. Thus, whenever possible, connect your Actions during CAR stories with "buts" and "therefores" to ensure that the *story* part of a CAR story is not lost!

Can I use the same story twice, but highlight different Actions the second time around?

This isn't a great look.

Employers see a dozen or so bullet points on your resume, and they really have time to ask you for only five or so stories during a thirty-minute interview, so the fact that you double-dip into a story you've already told will make them question the credibility of your other accomplishments—similar to how you'd be skeptical of a job applicant who says, "I know you asked for three references, but are you open to accepting just two this time?" Something will seem off.

Thus, don't do this. There's always a chance it could make an interviewer suspicious, whereas a brand-new story never will.

OK, I understand the Cherry-Pick; how does our second approach, the Ready-to-Eat, work?

The Ready-to-Eat recognizes that most projects in any profession follow a standard process of three Actions:

1. Understand the challenge.
2. Brainstorm solutions.
3. Implement the best solution(s).

I call this the RTE (Ready-to-Eat) approach because the structure is already fully cooked, just like an RTE ration for the military or adventurists. All you need to do to "unwrap" your answer is fill in the specific steps you took for each of those three Action items.

My favorite thing about the RTE is that a laundry list of completed tasks *is* acceptable when presented within an overarching Action, like understanding the problem or developing solutions. When ten Actions are laundry-listed without any overarching structure, your approach will seem chaotic rather than thoughtful; however, with an overarching structure, you will reassure your interviewer that your success was more or less guaranteed.

Reassure my interviewer? How?

They will recognize that you had a strategy. If any one of your individual steps had failed, you had tried other avenues to (for example) understand the problem. The odds of *all* of those steps failing are slim, so they know you would still have gotten the job done even if a setback or mishap had been encountered along the way.

Huh?

Let's look at an example of the RTE in action by answering the question "Tell me about a time where you had to solve an ambiguously scoped problem?"

> *One of my consulting clients was told by Wall Street to reduce their Days Sales Outstanding (DSO) figure, a measure of the time it took for them to receive payment from customers. My role was to optimize their standard client contracts to reduce DSO [CHALLENGE].*
>
> *There were three main actions I took to address this problem. The first action was to gain a better understanding of this issue [ACTION #1]. To do so, I learned as much as I could from internal experts regarding reducing DSO, interviewed sales agents from the client to learn what their goals were in drafting a contract with a client, and reviewed many existing contracts to see if I could identify any best practices. My biggest finding was that some payments were due thirty days from receipt of the invoice rather than invoice date. This ensured most payments would show up as uncollected across two calendar months instead of just one, which would double their DSO figure.*
>
> *Thus, my second action was to design a new contract template [ACTION #2]. I took one of the better contracts from the sales team and applied all of the best practices I'd identified to it—including the one about tying payment due dates to invoice date rather than receipt date—to create a new template, ensuring that all new and renegotiated contracts would meet Wall Street's guidance from a DSO perspective.*
>
> *However, I needed to get support for the new template, so my third action was to get everyone on board with my proposed solution [ACTION #3]. To do so, I showed my new contract template first to my supervisor to get his support, and then to our client team lead to get hers as well. Then I introduced it to the client's buyers, along with an Excel "wizard" that allowed buyers*

(and their supervisors) to enter a contract's terms to determine whether it was compliant with management's DSO targets.

*As a **RESULT**, the new contract was adopted, and the company's DSO was projected to drop by 20 percent within the first year, and then by 50 percent within five years as old contracts expired and were replaced by the new template.*

You can see from the answer that under each Action, there were several sub-steps listed, as in this chart:

ACTION 1: UNDERSTAND THE PROBLEM	ACTION 2: DESIGN A SOLUTION	ACTION 3: IMPLEMENT A SOLUTION
a. Consulted internal DSO experts.	a. Identified best existing contract template.	a. Gained support of supervisor and client leads.
b. Interviewed client's sales agents.	b. Modified it to create new contract template.	b. Designed Excel wizard.
c. Reviewed existing contracts.		c. Demo'd wizard for buyers.

Laundry lists within an overarching goal, such as understanding the problem, are acceptable. Laundry lists without overarching goals seem random and disorganized and are therefore discouraged.

If you do find yourself wanting to mention all ten Actions you took to overcome a Challenge, the RTE approach would be your best option.

So the Actions make sense, but what do I need to know about Results?

The only thing to keep in mind here is that interview questions allow you more real estate to discuss qualitative Results from your Actions than resume bullets, where space is more limited.

So be sure to mention the qualitative benefits of the work you did. If, in our example, the new contract template reduced buyer anxiety about getting management support for new contracts, that is completely appropriate to mention during a CAR story, even though it likely would not fit in your resume's bullet point. The more Results you can cite from your work, the better.

In fact, if you have thirty seconds worth of Results to discuss from your CAR story, take the full thirty seconds and trim down your Challenge and Actions, accordingly, since Results are what most quickly earn you serious consideration from interviewers.

So how many of these CAR stories will I actually use?

You should use your five favorite CAR stories in nearly every interview. They are your best stories, so you should make sure your interviewer has the opportunity to hear them.

At two minutes each, these five stories will take you about ten minutes to tell in total. Add in thirty seconds per question for the interviewer to take notes and ask you the next question, plus five minutes for small talk and about two minutes each for three (on average) of the Big Four, and you're already twenty-five minutes into the interview! Most interviewers will want to leave you at least five minutes in a thirty-minute interview to ask them questions, so five stories may be all you need.

For a forty-five-minute interview, you may be asked an additional story or two, but you are also likely to have ten minutes to pose questions to your interviewer; we'll discuss what to ask at the end of interviews in the next chapter.

Is there anything else I should add to my CAR Matrix besides just summaries of my Challenge, Actions, and Results?

Yes! As you practice your stories to ensure that you can deliver them in two minutes each time you tell them, you will identify certain phrases that just sound really good. Perhaps you find a way to capture a complex idea in just a few words, or you identify an alliterative phrase that just makes your story more fun to listen to. In any case, *write these phrases down word-for-word in your CAR Matrix.*

I call these "guidepost phrases." Much as guideposts help you know that you're heading in the right direction during a hike or car trip, guidepost phrases reassure you that your CAR stories are running on track and on time. They give you a moment of relaxation mid-answer, since you're about to say a phrase you enjoy and that you know lands well with your audiences. In short, they are phrases that put a smile on your face.

They are also phrases you will use every single time you tell the story. That said, they are the *only* phrases you will repeat verbatim every time you tell the story!

A common complaint I've heard from interviewers is that candidates sound too robotic and memorized during interviews. Reciting an answer entirely from memory actually takes a lot of cognitive energy, so job seekers who adopt this approach have spent so much effort trying to remember what words to use that they forget there's a human being seeking connection and authenticity on the other side of the conversation. It's like listening to an automated customer service hotline for the interviewer at that point: tedious, impersonal, and frustrating. Thus, memorizing your entire answer is not an option, and besides, memorizing every CAR story verbatim is no way to go through life; it's a brutal and unnecessary amount of work. Instead, just memorize the major elements: Challenge, Actions, Results, and guidepost phrases.

Success in interviews is not just about saying the right words in the right order. It's about keeping your listener engaged. If you, the interviewee, don't care about this story, your interviewer won't either.

I've entered all my CAR stories into my CAR Matrix, but I'm missing relevant stories for a few questions! *Now* what do I do?

I recommend looking at your old job descriptions and performance reviews to spur recall of times when you may have demonstrated a less-used skill to see if that sparks your memory about an applicable story.

What if they ask something I've never heard before, like "Describe a time when you turned a stranger into an advocate to complete a project"?

Great question! (And great question! I'm totally using that one in my next interview!)

Indeed, there is no way you can predict *every* question an employer will throw at you during an interview, so you will need to improvise from time to time.

However, *under no circumstances* should you try to improvise a CAR story during an interview! This never turns out well. Invariably, your timing will be way off, or you'll get lost in the details of your story, or you'll come off as unpracticed or unprofessional.

Do I just say "Pass" in that case?

I wish! Sadly, no.

First, ask them for a moment to think so you can choose the best story to answer their question. Sometimes just taking five to ten extra seconds to think helps you realize that one of your existing CAR stories answers that question better than you might have initially thought, and if not, then it will give you a chance to diagnose what generally appealing skill the interviewer is inquiring about (perhaps, here, the ability to influence others). In other words, can a little extra time help you figure out why they're asking this question?

If not, pick the CAR story you think comes *closest* to answering the question and go with that, but tell it about fifteen seconds faster than normal, since the version of it that you will tell *this* time will be a CART story.

What's a CART story?

It's a CAR story with a Takeaway (the T in CART) added at the end.

Takeaways are unifying thoughts added to the end of CAR stories when you *revisit the original question* and very explicitly explain how your story answers that question. In this example, your Takeaway would start with "The reason this is my favorite example of gaining someone's confidence quickly to complete a project is ____," filling in the blank as sincerely and effectively as you can.

Why is *that* better than trying to tell a CAR story for the first time in an interview?

If you choose to come up with a new CAR story during an interview, you are *immediately* improvising from the moment the question is asked, and for a full two minutes. If you convert a well-practiced CAR story into a CART story for an unexpected question like our example here, you're improvising for only the final *15* seconds rather than the full 120. Furthermore, you get 105 seconds of telling a familiar, comfortable story to be internally thinking of a way that this story *does* actually answer the question.

Does that actually work?

Yes, it does. Just ask any strategy consultant.

Remember the Rule of Three we discussed in the last chapter? It's a common joke among and about strategy consultants that they will often start answers in a Rule of Three format (as in "There are three main reasons why . . .") while having only *two* reasons in mind, but with full confidence that they'll think of a third reason by the time they're done talking. (I'm no exception; old habits die hard!)

The point is, I'd rather you improvise for fifteen seconds at the end of an answer after having nearly two minutes to think of a Takeaway, rather than improvise for a full two minutes starting immediately. Plus, while talking through your story, you are likely to stumble upon a detail or two that you realize allows you to tie back your answer to the original question at the end.

For example, if Aditya received this question and—not having a better story to answer it with—decided to use his aforementioned DSO reduction CAR story, Aditya might realize, mid-story, that he *did* actually have to turn strangers into advocates when he sold his new contract template idea to his client's buyers to get their support (part of his third Action).

This would give him more than enough information to create an effective Takeaway, such as "The reason this is my favorite example of turning a stranger into an advocate on demand is that my client's buyers were initially very skeptical of me because I was an outside consultant, but by showing them how the new contract template was in their own best interests—by helping them both improve their annual bonuses (through faster client payments) and maintain the company stock price so their options had more value—I was able to turn these potential adversaries into ardent allies."

Now, turning strangers into advocates wasn't the sole focus of Aditya's CAR story, but *most* of our greatest-hit CAR stories demonstrate multiple positive qualities, so pulling out one particular element for a Takeaway is totally acceptable, particularly in response to an unfamiliar or unexpected interview question.

Am I restricted to using Takeaways only when I'm asked unfamiliar questions?

Absolutely not! You could include Takeaways for every single interview question you are asked, if that is your preference.

The nice thing about Takeaways is they allow you to revisit the interviewer's question at the very end of your story so they know you were listening and that you answered the question they asked. Plus, it allows you to make explicit the connection between their question and your story. Sometimes that connection may seem obvious to you but not to your interviewer, and interviewers' minds *do* wander, so never trust them to connect the dots; if there are dots to connect, you should do it for them explicitly.

Finally, Takeaways are just kind of fun. They allow you to "put a bow" on your answer, shifting from a story that you've rehearsed a number of times to a completely organic and natural summary that addresses their specific question.

That said, Takeaways do take some time out of your two allotted minutes per answer, and they can sound a bit forced if used for *every* question. Thus, I like reserving them just for (1) when you're not confident that your CAR story perfectly answers their question, so you can clarify how it *does* connect, or (2) when they ask you for superlatives, like "What is your proudest accomplishment?" or "What is your biggest strength?"

Am I supposed to use a CAR story when they ask me my biggest strength? Couldn't I just tell them what my biggest strength is?

Let's try it out. Let's say your biggest strength is "communication skills."

Now what do you say?

Say nothing, and if your interviewer does likewise, the ensuing dead air will immediately sabotage your answer, just as saying "Everyone says I'm funny" all but proves that you're not. Clearly you'd want to provide some supporting evidence to prove that you have good communication skills.

You could speak generally about how you're good at communicating, but that will seem squishy and unsubstantial. I'd recommend just keeping interview life easy on yourself and proving that strength through a tried-and-true CAR story. (If you're genuinely not sure that a CAR story is welcome, definitely ask, "Would you like an example?")

It might feel as if you're missing a chance to just have a normal conversation with your interviewer about your biggest strength, but (1) *they* may not be seeking a genuine conversation about your biggest strength, preferring instead to see some evidence of that strength in action, and (2) your Takeaway at the end allows you to finish on a genuine, customized note. Aditya, for example, could finish his DSO story this way: "The biggest thing I've learned about effective communication is to think like your audience before choosing what to say. What information will *the buyers*—not their bosses, nor Wall Street, nor the consultants—find most compelling? By focusing on that first and foremost, I can get people nodding in agreement, and the rest usually falls into place."

Sometimes interviewers ask for a list, though, like "What are your three biggest strengths?" How do I answer those?

Still with a CAR story—*maybe*. It depends on your interviewer's preference.

In this case, my recommendation is to answer authentically. Don't think in terms of what stories you haven't used yet—just give them what you consider your three biggest strengths. They may jump in with a follow-up. If they toss you a softball like "What do those strengths mean to you?" that's a signal that you can just speak generally about your strengths. But they may get specific and ask you for a CAR story, with "Can you give me an example of where you put those three strengths in action?"

If they don't jump in with a follow-up, I recommend you ask them if they'd like an example. They will probably say yes, or they wouldn't have allowed you to pause after you listed your three favorite strengths. In this case, either pick a story that you know incorporates those three elements (which I suspect will be difficult for you to do on the fly) or, barring that magical "aha!" moment, select your favorite CAR story that you have not yet told, but with the intent to include a Takeaway at the end connecting each of the top three strengths that you named to the actions you took or behaviors you demonstrated.

For example, Aditya demonstrated more than just three strengths during his example from earlier; name any three positive qualities or attributes, and Aditya could likely find examples of them somewhere in that story: perseverance, positivity, problem-solving, and so on.

As we learned way back in chapter 1, our top Strengths are more about *how* we do things than *what* we do. It's our internal computer code; our order of operations for tackling difficult problems. Thus it's likely our biggest strengths pop up, one way or another, in our preferred CAR stories.

But sometimes employers ask me about *negative* traits—how do I answer *those* questions?

I recommend, again, using CAR stories, but this is where things can get a bit tricky. Thankfully, these questions tend to arrive later in interviews (after the fifteen-minute mark)—well after the point when most interviewers have made up their mind—so don't let these throw you off too badly.

It's critical to note here that even though employers are asking you about *negative* qualities and experiences—like failures, mistakes, and weaknesses—they are still seeking information on your positive traits, like resilience, responsibility, or professionalism. "Seeking massive screw-up with management aspirations" said no employer ever.

The two common errors job seekers make when faced with these questions is to become defensive and to dwell on negatives for the full two-minute duration of their answers. For the former case, you need to keep in mind that interviewers aren't evaluating your former colleagues; they are evaluating *you*. For the latter case, all the things you did wrong won't help your case any; how you made amends or prevented future instances *will* help.

You have a couple of strategic options for how to answer this question. I recommend choosing whichever feels more authentic to you.

The first is the more traditional: create a CAR story specifically *for* negatively framed questions. This may or may not be a CAR story you have already created. I recommend reviewing the stories currently in your CAR Matrix. Would any be suitable for answering "Tell me about a time you failed," for example? Sometimes setbacks lead us into some of our most notable accomplishments, but we typically omit these negative origin stories when telling positive CAR stories. If you identify one of your CAR stories that could be reframed as bouncing back from a failure, absolutely embrace that. Simply mention the negative origins of that CAR story in your Challenge, whereas in other questions you would simply leave those unstated (unless of course mentioning said setbacks in your Challenge enhances the impressiveness of your eventual Results).

However, many of us don't have a plug-and-play CAR story in which a mistake that we had omitted can now be mentioned in response to a negatively framed question. If this is you, you may need to craft a CAR story around a genuine mistake that you made and the systematic approach you took to repair that error. You should create this like any other CAR story, but confine the failure to the Challenge. Focus your Actions on how you made amends; the Results should summarize how you fixed the error to the best of your ability—*ideally*, this should involve turning lemons into lemonade, with your initial failure ending up leading to success anyway.

What if I don't have any failure stories where I turned lemons into lemonade and achieved success anyway?

Then the second option I have for you may prove more appealing.

I call it a SCAR story. It's the mirror image of a CART story. In a CART story, you add a takeaway to an existing CAR story to help it answer an unexpected or superlative question. In a SCAR story, you introduce a Setback that helps you pivot into an existing CAR story.

But isn't that just like including a setback in the Challenge of a CAR story?

Not quite. In that approach, your Setback is part of the same immediate story. You made a mistake, and you were able to successfully fix it. In a SCAR story, your Setback comes from a *different* story or work experience—ideally from earlier in your career—which gave you the wisdom to help you perform better in a future iteration of a similar problem (an existing CAR story, ideally).

The benefit of this approach is twofold: first, if you don't have a "happily ever after" example of fixing a mistake to everyone's more-than-satisfaction, it gives you a story where you don't have to just play defense for two minutes; and second, it allows you to use an already-practiced, *positive* CAR story as your pivot. In other words, you use the Setback to acknowledge a failure from earlier in your career, but you use the Challenge to pivot to a better story where you incorporated the lessons you learned from your earlier mishap. A phrase like "Thankfully, I had a shot at redemption on my next project, where I . . ."

Everyone has encountered failure in their career. In some cases, we are able to impressively recover from our mistakes (our first approach), but in others, we must simply clean up the mess as best we can and learn from the experience, doing our best to prevent a similar scenario from ever happening again (or at least minimizing its likelihood with the benefit of newfound hindsight). In *that* case, I prefer SCAR stories.

What's wrong with just admitting that you learned from a failure?

Nothing in and of itself, but in an interview setting, you don't want to resort to making promises to potential future employers.

Remember, when employers ask you about negative circumstances, they are seeking positive attributes. When your story in its entirety consists of admitting a failure and how you learned from it, that definitely demonstrates thoughtfulness, which is critical but incomplete, since thoughtfulness alone is not exactly a complete meal; it's the equivalent of saying you're going to go on a diet tomorrow while eating an entire pizza, but not actually having identified which diet you're going on, what groceries you need to procure, what your exercise routine will be, or any other actionable details. It's aspirational rather than operational.

Thus our answers should include both an acknowledgment of failure and either a thorough turnaround that leads to a happy ending (our first approach), an actual example of improvement in the future (our SCAR story approach), or at worst a plan of attack for improvement for the future (the "I've researched a number of different diets and I am planning to start Tim Ferriss's *The 4-Hour Body* slow-carb diet tomorrow, since it allows me one cheat day a week—and two glasses of red wine per night to help me overlook the pain of being on a low-carb diet").

Back to Aditya's example: if asked "Tell me about a time you failed," he could turn his CAR story into a SCAR story by opening with a Setback from earlier in his career, like this:

> *During my first year as an analyst, I had spent hours creating a presentation outlining our team's recommendations for our client. However, I hadn't shown this presentation to my colleagues on the client side in advance, so my presentation was quickly derailed by their questions and objections to the plan they were seeing for the first time [SETBACK]. I realized the error of my ways, made many apologies to my client for blindsiding them, and promised myself I would never again fail to get my team's buy-in before elevating recommendations to my supervisors.*

Thankfully, I had a shot at redemption on my next project, when I was tasked with improving a client's DSO figure [CHALLENGE], which Wall Street had criticized as being too high . . .

And with that, Aditya transitions into the rest of his CAR story, trimming its details around his first two Actions and focusing intently on his third Action, building support among his client colleagues before making further recommendations.

If desired, and if time permitted, Aditya could even choose to add a Takeaway to this story, highlighting his learning from the experience that an ounce of prevention is worth a pound of cure when gaining buy-in for initiatives, especially when those initiatives involve changes to how people perform their jobs.

Would you then call that a SCART story?

(Sigh.) Yes, but not proudly. Even *I* have limits when it comes to acronyms.

Well, what if my interviewer asks me about my biggest weakness instead of my biggest failure? Is that basically the same question?

They are very similar, but failure questions are actually easier to answer, since failures are in the past, while weaknesses are ongoing.

What do you mean?

Well, if Aditya had told his previous SCART (gah!) story, it's very possible his interviewer could counter with "Well, it sounds like gaining buy-in from your teammates is no longer a weakness."

Whereas making a full recovery from a Setback is acceptable (and preferred) in failure questions, a full recovery isn't allowed in weakness questions—you must still be a work in progress, or else you've failed to answer the question.

Don't sweat this, though. That's what the Takeaway is for.

Had Aditya been asked "What is your biggest weakness?" he could have started his answer with "Sometimes in my desire to turn my ideas into action, I fail to bring along my teammates. For example, during my first year as an analyst . . ." and he's back into his SCART story. However, to preserve the integrity of the question, his Takeaway following his story would have to point out a shortcoming of his solution to demonstrate that he is still a work in progress rather than fully recovered, such as:

> *While the project was successful, it was not perfect. My client's buyers were slow to buy in, and I realize now it was because I never involved them in the template improvement brainstorming process [SHORTCOMING]. On my next project involving consensus-building, I will ensure I am more inclusive and invite anyone impacted by my work to share their opinions so that everyone is invested in a positive outcome [TAKEAWAY].*

What if they ask me about a *hypothetical* negative scenario, like "How would you handle a situation where you disagreed with your boss?"

These are called *situational questions*, and they seem to be becoming more popular recently, according to my students and other job seekers I work with.

One option is to simply answer as honestly and authentically as possible. If you are a good communicator and you can speak off the cuff in an organized fashion, then this approach would be totally appropriate.

However, some of us struggle with clarity when we speak extemporaneously; our thoughts can come out sounding a bit scattered and hard to follow, like the "and then" answers we discussed in the last chapter. "I would do this, and then I would do this, and then I would do this." Thankfully, there's a better way, and it's one we've already learned. Remember the RTE approach from earlier? Thankfully, that format works *very* well for situational questions as well.

In most hypothetical situations you'd be presented with, you'd first want to understand the problem: for example, you might ask your boss questions to ensure you fully understand *their* perspective before explaining your own. Second, you'd want to design some solutions: perhaps you'd take some time to identify solutions that give all stakeholders a quick win. Third, you'd want to implement your ideas: maybe you set up a brainstorming session on the topic, so your broader team can workshop your initial proposals and maybe identify new, superior ones.

Understand, design, implement. That simple structure can allow you to address any hypothetical situation in an organized (and Rule of Three–friendly) fashion!

What if they ask me about a time I faced an ethical dilemma?

Ouch. In my opinion, this is the single toughest question you'll face in an interview. Thankfully, it doesn't come up often, but you should still be prepared for it.

What if I've never faced an ethical dilemma?

We've *all* faced ethical dilemmas where any course of action would hurt *somebody*. Perhaps you instituted a policy that was inconvenient for your colleagues but reduced your organization's risk, or you found a bargain but had to decide whether to make a major purchase decision without consulting your boss or spouse first. In any case, these tend to be situations we don't love remembering, since there's no clear-cut right answer, by definition.

So that leaves us with a couple of options.

First, if you were a heroic whistleblower in the past and took one for the team to save the company, now would be the time to tell that story! However, most of us don't have an ethical superhero moment to fall back on so . . .

Second, it's important to remember that employers are seeking positive behaviors even when they ask you about negative circumstances. When interviewers ask about ethical dilemmas, they are seeking good judgment, a moral code, and candor.

Thus you need to identify a story where there truly was no right answer. For example, did you ever identify an action that would have helped a few people but caused panic in many more? Or one where making an exception to help a well-meaning individual may set an unsustainable precedent for less well-meaning ones in the future?

Once again, the RTE structure works well for bringing order to chaos. How did you (1) understand the problem, (2) design the least-bad solution available, and (3) implement that idea as sensitively as possible?

Try to have a CAR story reserved in your CAR Matrix just for this one. It won't be a story you'll tell often, but it will be there for you just in case.

Anything else I need to know?

Not really. Behavioral interviews are pretty formulaic. Interviewers want to hear examples of positive attributes, and there are only so many ways to probe for those in the limited time they will devote to such questions.

Furthermore, keep in mind that fewer than one out of five (17.7 percent) of interviews are decided during the behavioral stage. Here's a chart of the stats I shared in the last chapter:

INTERVIEW TIME ELAPSED (MIN)	% OF INTERVIEWS DECIDED	CUMULATIVE % DECIDED	TYPICAL INTERVIEW CONTENT
0 to 1	4.9%	4.9%	First impression, small talk
1 to 5	25.5%	30%	Small talk (cont.), TMAY
5 to 15	29.5%	60%	TMAY (cont.), the Big Four
Over 15	17.7%	78%	Behavioral interview questions; "What questions do you have for me?" (see chapter 6)
Post-interview	22.5%	100%	Thank-you note

So please don't freak out about CAR stories. Just commit to doing your best (and to making a CAR Matrix—I can't overstress the importance of this!). If you want to freak out about anything, freak out about the Big Four.

In the next chapter we'll cover "What questions do you have for me?" Then we'll move on to what to do after the interview!

CHAPTER CHECKLIST

Do you have ten to fifteen CAR stories in your CAR Matrix? ✓

Do you have at least one CAR story per skill, trait, or experience you expect employers to ask you about? ✓

Can you deliver each of your ten to fifteen CAR stories in two minutes? ✓

Do you have Results for every one of your CAR stories? ✓

Can you turn your CAR stories into CART stories when asked unfamiliar or superlative behavioral interview questions? ✓

Do you have SCAR or SCART stories prepared for failure and/or weakness questions? ✓

Are you prepared to describe an ethical dilemma you've faced? ✓

TROUBLESHOOTING

What if I don't have that much work experience, so I can't come up with ten to fifteen professional CAR stories?

In that case, feel free to create CAR stories from your personal, social (as in volunteer or community activities), or academic life that demonstrate the skills or traits your potential employers are likely to ask you about.

Even if you are a professional with *many* years of experience, mixing in a personal, social, or academic story can be a nice change of pace, demonstrating you are a real person rather than just a corporate drone.

I've heard that some employers ask case interview questions—how do I answer those?

These are too complex and industry/sector-specific to fit into this book. However, even case interviews will feature one or more of the Big Four and some behavioral interview questions as well, so this book will still be of use to you.

If you suspect you'll be asked case questions in an upcoming interview, though, I highly recommend getting a book that covers case interviews in your sector in more detail to prepare for that specific portion of your interview.

CHAPTER 7

What Questions Do You Have for Me?

Do we really need a chapter on this?

Yes, because of the peak-end rule.

What's the peak-end rule?

The peak-end rule states that people rate an experience based on a combination of two moments—the experience's most intense moment and the final moment of the experience—rather than an average of every moment of the experience.

Behavioral economist Daniel Kahneman, author of *Thinking, Fast and Slow*, identified this phenomenon in a rather uncomfortable way. He found that colonoscopy patients who were randomly selected to have the scope remain in their bodies for three extra minutes without movement, in which the sensation would be uncomfortable but not painful as during other parts of the exam, rated the exam less painful than patients who underwent the normal exam and had the scope removed three minutes earlier—but with no "rest" period afterward.[1]

Kahneman found that the duration of the experience didn't change people's rating of it, curiously. Just how it felt at its most intense and *how it felt at the end.*

Interviews are (marginally) less uncomfortable than colonoscopies, but the peak-end rule should still be on our radar, just as it is for pugilists trying to leave a good last impression for the judges when they go for broke at the end of a round.

We can't control what our interviewers will consider the peak moment of our interview, but we can make sure we adhere to expectations during the interview's closing moments so the interviewer finds our end behavior comfortable rather than unusual.

Giving them back some time in their day would be a pleasant end to an interview, right? Can't I just not have any questions?

No. For an interviewer, getting time back in their day is nice, but having a candidate end an interview awkwardly by having no questions is worse and definitely violates the peak-end rule. Thus we need to have at least several questions prepared. In fact, I've experienced an *entire interview* (only once, thankfully) where the interviewer turned it over to me for questions starting from the opening moments!

How did you manage an interview where you had to come up with all the questions?

I started with the handful of questions I had prepared for the interview, and then I scrambled to just keep my interviewer talking so I wouldn't have to come up with any new ones. "Oh, a factory that *only* makes rubber pellets? Please *go on.*"

In retrospect, I would have managed it more like an informational meeting, using the TIARA Framework I outlined in *The 2-Hour Job Search.* Essentially, you frame the interviewer as an expert in their field for the first half of the interview by asking questions about Trends they're encountering and Insights they've had along the way. Then I'd pivot to framing them as a mentor by asking what Advice they'd give themself if they were in my shoes today, what Resources they'd recommend I look into next to learn more, and what Assignments (or projects) they found most impactful. This takes them on a logical journey that first establishes likability, then primes creativity, and then requests empathy; that process maximizes the chance that you can systematically turn a stranger into an ally over the course of a single informational meeting, and a job interview where you manage the full agenda is essentially an informational meeting. Can you use this person's time wisely?

However, this is an exceptionally rare case. Just know that it does happen, and having a plan for such a topsy-turvy interview will increase your confidence in all other, more normal interviews!

So use this time to learn as much as you can from an expert in the field. Typically, your simple act of deference to use your time to learn rather than self-promote will spur greater interest on the part of your interviewer, and you will find (as I did so many years ago) that "interested is interesting," meaning your genuine interest in them results in their genuine interest in you.

In addition, after reading this chapter, you will know to have some "expensive" (my term for heavily researched) questions you've prepared in advance. Work those in as well to demonstrate that you did your homework on the employer before the interview, in case you get the sense they're focused more on how you prepared for the interview rather than on how well you form rapport with a stranger, since different interviewers do tend to want different things. The best we can do is "aim for the middle of the fairway," since it is not possible to be all things to all people; we can just be sure to have different clubs in our bag so we're prepared for any situation.

So, that is the hardest possible scenario you could ever face with respect to "What questions do you have for me?" If you can handle *that*, you can handle anything.

Next, let's face the more common scenarios. For the rest of this chapter, we'll talk about how to handle this question, as the time remaining in the interview at the point this question is asked increases from zero to the most common duration, which is from five minutes (for thirty-minute interviews) to fifteen minutes (for hour-long interviews).

Sounds good. So what do I choose to ask if this question comes while they're walking me out the door?

There is one question you must *always* ask, even if the interview time is up and you are on your way out. That question is "When will I hear back regarding my status in this process?"

This question is for *you*. I can't even tell you how many times I have seen job seekers panic for days, weeks, and even months after an interview because they failed to ask this one simple question. In some cases, that panic was well warranted. The decision had gone out within twenty-four hours to those who received offers, but the declined candidates never heard back either way (which is a truly *awful* thing for an employer to do to a candidate, but it happens—regularly).

The point is, if you don't ask when you'll hear more, you don't know when to follow up. And I *always* recommend following up. It is the least I would expect from a genuinely interested job seeker.

Now, if the projected response time they gave you passes without any word, it's possible that some important people were out sick and decisions were delayed, or that decisions had gone out to those receiving offers but not the rest yet. Either way, it will give you peace of mind just to know when further follow-up from you is justified. We'll talk more about how to follow up on interviews where you have not yet received a decision in the next chapter.

In summary, if you get only one question at the end of the interview, make absolutely sure that it is "When will I hear back regarding my status in this process?"

OK, so what if they ask me "What questions do you have for me?" with about five minutes left in the interview?

To me, this leaves you time to ask "When will I hear back regarding my status in this process?" followed by one more question, and I recommend making this question either a rapport-building question, an expensive question (again, that's my term for a question that proves you've done your research), or a Research and Rapport (R&R) question that offers the best of both worlds.

The general formula for an R&R question is "I read about [relevant trend in this employer's space] in [reputable source]. Has that impacted you and your work? If so, how?"

The benefit is it not only demonstrates you did your homework before the interview, but also frames the question in a manner where the interviewer can't lose face, meaning they can't be embarrassed by their lack of knowledge. Ideally, the trend you cite will be global enough that it will impact everyone at that employer in some way, but if not, the worst they can say is "That is an important situation, but it really hasn't impacted *my* work at all," to which you can follow up with a classic TIARA Trend question like "Well, what macro trend *is* most impacting your work right now?"—which again is a question they can answer with 100-percent authority, rather than being concerned they may get the question "wrong."

Too often, in job seekers' fervor for demonstrating their research, I see them play "stump the recruiter" by asking an overly detailed question that the interviewer won't have personally encountered. Therefore, don't be too esoteric in your questions, and make sure it calls not for a fact (which they may or may not correctly know) but for their *opinion* (a topic on which each of us is the world's foremost expert, regardless of what's been asked!).

By asking them a question that they are the best-qualified person in the world to answer (and which they can't get wrong), you'll ensure you manage the end part of the peak-end rule by asking them a question that amounts to "Why *are* you so smart at your job?"—leaving any interviewer with a self-satisfied glow.

Makes sense. But what if they leave me ten to fifteen minutes of time for questions?

Again, you'll start with the "next steps" question so you don't forget, and it may prompt follow-up questions, so you'll want to be sure to leave ample time. Then, instead of compressing everything into one R&R question, you can focus more exclusively on rapport-building with an R&R question tossed in to prove you did your homework.

Why wouldn't I just ask all R&R questions?

Fair question. R&R questions tend to take a decent amount of time to come up with (I'd say about fifteen minutes each), and I'm going to assume you don't have unlimited time to prepare for this interview.

Having just a couple of R&R questions ready to go heading into an interview will suffice. The rest should be pure rapport building, and I'd alternate between them to see to which the interviewer responds to more positively. (Generally, a positive reaction is indicated by an increased level of energy, so if they seem energized by your question, ask more like that!)

Examples of more pure rapport-building questions are the Trends, Insights, and Advice questions from the TIARA Framework that I mentioned earlier. Trend questions are ones like "How do you think this job will be most different five years from now?" Insight questions are ones like "What do you know now about your employer or this sector that you wish you knew when you were in my position just starting out?" Finally, Advice questions are ones like "If you were me, what is the one thing you would be doing right now to best prepare for a career in this field/at this organization?"

These questions require no research, and they are not ones you can find the answers to on the internet; if you ask these questions of ten people, you will get ten different answers, and every single one will be correct. Furthermore, there is no chance of playing "stump the recruiter" here, because, as we discussed earlier, you are asking them for just their opinions rather than black-and-white facts.

And that's all there is to know about "What questions do you have for me?"! I told you it would be a short chapter, but because of the peak-end rule, it's critical you don't take this question lightly!

Do you have the ability to manage a job interview as if it were an informational (if the interviewer has no prepared questions for you)? ✓

Do you know to ask "When will I hear back regarding my status in this process?" at the end of *every* interview? ✓

Do you have multiple R&R-style questions to ask if you detect your interviewer prefers research-based questions? ✓

Do you have rapport-building questions drawn from the TIARA Framework if you sense your interviewer prefers rapport-based questions? ✓

TROUBLESHOOTING

I'm a member of a marginalized community, so finding a safe, supportive, and inclusive work environment is critical to me. However, I don't know when or how to ask about this. Is the end of an interview an appropriate time? If so, how do I ask? If not, when?

This is indeed important.

I recommend asking these questions during informationals preceding an interview rather than at the end of the interview, simply because they are too important to rush. Furthermore, your interviewer may not have informed answers, so resolving these questions may take a few attempts. You may find during your informationals alone that this organization is not one you can thrive in, making interviewing with them undesirable and unnecessary.

That said, if you are unable to get these questions answered before your interview and it is unclear whether your interviewer would possess relevant information regarding the experience of marginalized employees at their organization, I recommend saving them for *after* the interview—specifically, after you have received an offer. At this point, the organization is highly incentivized to get you the information you are seeking, so you can be very honest about what you need to feel comfortable joining their team.

What if my interviewer says, "I don't know when you'll hear more about your status in this process"?

If they do not offer you a firm timeline—for example, they say, "I don't really know. That's out of my hands, but someone should get back to you soon"—then try to identify a firm timeline *for identifying a firm timeline,* as in "Thank you for that! If I don't hear from anyone for a couple of weeks, should I follow up with you or someone else?"

A couple of weeks should be *plenty* of time for any employer to have an update regarding your status—even if that update is that they need more time—and it will help you avoid most needless instances of being accidentally forgotten about, since you can follow up with a trusty "As promised, I wanted to check in with you after a couple of weeks . . ." (More on that in the next chapter, though—you just have to invite yourself to check back in with them if they don't proactively offer that option to you.)

There's a concept called *commitment and consistency* that psychologist Robert Cialdini identified in his 1984 book *Influence.* In one study he cites, he found that bystanders who verbally agreed to watch a fellow beachgoer's things intervened to prevent a (simulated) robbery 95 percent of the time, whereas bystanders who gave no verbal commitment intervened just 20 percent of the time.[2]

So just getting a verbal commitment from someone to say they will respond in the future makes it far more likely they will actually get back to you—even if they may not want to! Take advantage of this quirk of psychology and enlist your interviewer to give you an update even if they can't give you a decision. It will help you preserve your sanity during this job search marathon!

PART 3

After the Interview

CHAPTER 8

Follow-Up, Negotiations, and Offer Decisions

How do I follow up on the interview I just conducted?

First off, immediately set a reminder in your calendar for a day before you were told you'd hear back regarding your status in the process. You are thinking clearly now; you won't be then if you haven't yet heard from them!

You'll need to follow up when that reminder triggers, but first and foremost, you need to write a thank-you note.

Do thank-you notes really matter? Won't it seem pretty transparent that the only reason I'm sending one is because I want the job?

Exactly. It lets your interviewer know you want the job.

Despite being stressed and anxious and nervous, you still kept your eyes on the prize and remembered there was a job to do, and that was to sincerely thank the interviewer for giving you a shot at that position.

For some interviewers, the thank-you note means nothing; for others, it means a lot. Remember that nearly a quarter of interviewers (22.5 percent) make up their minds *after* the interview. The thank-you note is your one chance to influence their behavior in your favor during that time period.

So what do I put in the thank-you note?

It really is the thought that counts, but if you want a formula, here is what I put in mine, and I think this model hits all the main points:

1. Thank them for their time and consideration.
2. Highlight the most memorable or insightful piece of information they shared.
3. Reiterate your interest in the role and that you look forward to hearing their decision.

You can also invite them to contact you if they have additional questions, but that's a matter of taste (and that approach will be what you use if you do not hear from them within the promised time frame; for some job seekers, offering that option a second time would be uncomfortable).

In total, these should clock in at under a hundred words. This is not the time to sell yourself; rather, you're expressing gratitude in an efficient manner.

I've heard I should send handwritten thank-you notes. What do you think of that?

I wish this advice would die in a fire. Just being real.

"It differentiates you" and "It shows how much you care" seem to be the main arguments for this approach, but the cons to me are much more convincing, namely: a handwritten thank-you note can take a week or more to arrive, which is long after most interview decisions are made; handwritten notes take time, money, and effort to prepare; and handwritten notes require employers to have a system for tracking stationery, whereas most just have systems for tracking email. The upside is uncertain, the downside is certain. Don't take such bets.

With a thank-you email, you get the vast majority of the benefit and can ensure it arrives in time for the interviewer to see (within twenty-four hours is the typical time frame that is considered appropriate) if they are in fact factoring thank-you notes into their decision.

Couldn't I send *both* an email thank-you note and a hard copy?

Just, ugh. There are vastly better ways to spend your time!

Only if sending handwritten thank-you notes is, like, your "signature move" should you send both; otherwise, an email thank-you note alone will suffice!

I think I'm set on thank-you notes. What is this about following up on my interview, though? Isn't the employer supposed to contact *me* about whether I got the job?

Supposed to, yes. Do they always? Definitely not.

I sadly don't have data on how often this happens, but anecdotally employers tend to give you no update disproportionately when you are a wait-list candidate. This is kind of an awful way to treat someone who is still in the running, yet it happens with startling frequency.

Following up with an employer at the date they stated (or just before that date, which is my preference, to remove any awkwardness about their having already missed their own deadline) may not increase your odds of getting the offer, but it definitely won't hurt you, since it allows you to reiterate your interest, whereas less-interested candidates would disappear without even checking in. At worst, it will grant you a measure of goodwill and peace of mind regarding your status in the process, sparing you several weeks' worth of self-debate, trying to guess whether today is the right day to follow up . . . or would tomorrow be better?

Either way, don't feel bad! This potential missed deadline is on them. You are just trying to help them clean up after themselves.

How do I do *that* without looking like a jerk?

My preferred approach is to contact them by email a day before their stated deadline to thank them again for their consideration and to ask if you can provide any additional information that would facilitate their decision.

By following up shortly *before* the deadline, you don't put them in a situation where they lose face; you are giving them a chance to say "You beat me to this email! I was totally going to reach out to you this afternoon!" and everyone wins—you don't necessarily get the job, but you get an update and they feel good about their interaction with you, which helps keep you in the loop for any future positions that may open up, albeit not the one you interviewed for.

When job seekers wait until *after* the deadline to follow up, they invariably feel uncomfortable about it. "Am I going to annoy the employer?" or "They would have contacted me if they wanted to make me the offer, so I should just leave them alone, right?"

Don't do this to yourself. You need to preserve your energy at *every* step in the job search. Energy is a precious, finite resource, and waiting for people to ignore you is never a good place to spend that resource. Reach out before the deadline and save yourself that time expenditure while also demonstrating you are the type of candidate who asks for what they want, not the type who waits for things to break before acting.

What if they tell me I didn't get the offer?

Then at least you know, and you can free up that mental energy to pursue other opportunities.

It's not that following up with employers who are unresponsive after an interview is fun or even offers promising odds of success; it really just offers you closure, since an unresolved interview—even when the decision is already late—can offer you false hope, dampening your motivation to pursue other opportunities.

So what if I *get* the offer?

Then congratulations! That's wonderful! All of your hard work paid off!

Do I negotiate the offer?

Yes. Always, provided there is at least a non-zero percent chance you would accept it. Otherwise, save everyone that time.

When do I negotiate the offer?

I recommend beginning this process about a week before your deadline for accepting the offered position. Start later than that, and the process may extend beyond the deadline, which might vex your employer. Start earlier, and you risk losing a bit of leverage in three areas: negotiating power, personal brand, and optionality.

Regarding negotiating power: job seekers typically don't negotiate an offer unless they are seriously contemplating accepting. Thus, if you start negotiating immediately after receiving the offer, the employer knows you don't have other active options, which may reduce their motivation to improve their offer.

Regarding personal brand: once you have reached an endpoint in negotiations, employers will expect a decision, even if that is ahead of the official deadline. Thus, if you have other processes going on, hitting the brakes after it appeared the negotiation had resolved may alienate and embarrass any advocates who personally lobbied for your offer to be improved.

Even if you end up accepting, your delay may rub people the wrong way. They will clearly read this as your waiting for something better to come along instead of being excited to join.

Speaking of something better coming along, starting negotiations about a week before the deadline preserves your optionality. Especially if you have been following the process I outline in *The 2-Hour Job Search*, you'll know that offers seem to arrive in bunches and often unexpectedly. This happened to a graphic designer friend of mine who accepted his position before the stated deadline, only to have another offer that he preferred come along later that week.

These random late-game offers arise more frequently when you employ a broad networking campaign (as in *2HJS*) to secure your offer, so be especially careful about early-accepting if you have many advocates out there earnestly looking for opportunities on your behalf.

What if they don't offer me a week to decide? Or if I need more time to decide more generally?

You will definitely want to ask for an extension. That doesn't guarantee you'll get one, but the right logic and approach can go a long way to securing it.

You and your potential employer have aligned incentives here. You both want a good long-term fit. I've heard hiring managers say that it takes new hires a year before they become profitable, given all the time it takes to train you and get you up to speed. (Yes, summer interns, this means you are purely a money-loser during your stay there! They are using your internship as an extended interview and to advertise their company's brand to current and future students at your school.) They don't want to bring you in full time only to have you leave within a few months.

Presenting this logic to an employer is often enough to get you at least a weekend to think it over—nobody gets work done on Fridays anyway, right?

My preferred language for this is "May I please have the weekend to think it over? I just want to make sure I'm making the best possible long-term decision for both of us." Feel free to say this out loud verbatim if you're made an offer by phone or video giving you less than a week to decide.

What if they made the offer via email or voice mail—do I also email them my request to have the weekend to think?

No! Do *not* negotiate over email. *Ever*. Especially not over the time you have to make a decision. Imagine your email gets ignored. What then?

And this is not a hypothetical! Year after year, I know job seekers who ignore this guidance and who ask for extensions over email, and they simply never get a response as the deadline rapidly approaches. Not only are they freaking out, but they have a more pressing concern—do they refuse to *give* a decision when their deadline is about to pass?

Do *not* put yourself in this position.

I get it. Asking over email seems less uncomfortable than having this conversation, but that temporary convenience seems to invariably lead to longer-term discomfort and needless risk. Your email may get missed, or ignored, or forwarded, or laughed at. You just don't know! What you *do* know is that you'll panic in the interim, starting the very moment after you hit send.

So what do I do instead? Cold-call them and say I want to negotiate an extension?

You could, but there's an easier way that will get you a response even faster.

Simply email them to say you have a time-sensitive update regarding your status and you'd like to set up a call to discuss as soon as possible. (Note: Do not send this note on a weekend—the last thing you want here is to have a future boss set up a weekend call with you for a request they might have preferred to conduct during business hours!)

What if they don't respond to *that* message?

They always do! Not once in my fifteen-plus years as a career coach have I heard of such an email getting ignored (which is ironic, given how frequently negotiation and extension request emails seem to get "lost"). No, employers are *all over* clarifying what this one means.

The ambiguity of the request is what makes it so effective. The employer will not know whether you are asking for an extension or withdrawing from their process, and especially in the latter case they will want to know for sure so they can move on to other candidates as quickly as possible.

What if they ask me to state what the update is over email?

I'd simply say you'd prefer to discuss by phone so you could answer any questions in real time.

Over email, every "no" will seem definitive. During a phone call, you'll be able to detect that that "no" isn't as fixed as you think. If that "no" in person comes out more as a hedged "We'd really rather not, since we have this big project coming up, but if you absolutely *must have* the weekend to decide . . ." Bingo. However, you only get that meta-knowledge when you can hear their tone of voice. (This will also help us stay out of trouble with our prenegotiation call, which we'll discuss shortly.)

If they insist, then say in email that, sure, you'd like to discuss an extension. However, don't make this easy on them. If, after a couple of emails back and forth, they insist that you reveal that it's about an extension, they will have a much harder time ignoring your request after taking such an urgent, active interest in your time-sensitive update, so at worst you are reasonably ensured a prompt answer.

So what *if* they say no?

Then at least you *tried*, and in doing so—regardless of whether the "no" is in response to your asking for an extension or requesting to negotiate the offer—you've enhanced your brand.

If I hired ten people and only one tried to negotiate to get a better deal, that one person is definitely getting my most important project! I mean, if I can't trust my hires to negotiate on their own behalf, how can I trust them to negotiate on behalf of my company??

What if they rescind my offer because I tried to ask for an extension and/or negotiation?

The odds of this happening are incredibly low if you approach the topic sensitively.

That said, employers are very unlikely to make you their *best possible offer* in their first attempt. (There is one exception: if you are joining an employer where you would be part of a large starting class of people doing the same job. The most common example I see is interns at large employers, where the job assignments are so short that it's not worth opening Pandora's box to negotiate with any individual member of that start class.)

There are horror stories about rescinded offers from botched negotiation attempts, but in my many years of experience, these exceedingly rare instances are usually attributable to awkward or over-zealous approaches—exactly the opposite of what this book is preparing you for. In fact, I'm about to share with you my one custom-created technique—the prenegotiation call (or PNC)—that all but ensures that you'll know if there's flexibility in the offer before you even attempt to *start* negotiating.

What is a prenegotiation call?

The PNC is a call where you determine what is and is not negotiable in your offer. Note that *no actual negotiation* happens during this call. You would simply email your contact who made you the offer to request some time to discuss your offer, since you have some questions.

This requires that you have a written offer to review, so if one is not proactively furnished to you, you should request one before trying to conduct a PNC so you have something tangible to refer to.

What if my contact asks me to accept the offer before furnishing me with a written offer letter?

This is sketchy behavior, but it does happen—most often in investment banking, where recruiting teams are heavily evaluated based on their conversion rate of offers made to offers accepted. Thus, they don't want to make any offers that could be declined.

Thankfully, outside of that, it is relatively uncommon for an employer to express hesitancy about sending you a written offer.

More broadly, most employers wouldn't want their own employees to make a habit of accepting verbal contracts without seeing them in writing to make sure they are fully understood. So feel free to share that perspective with them as well while reiterating the sincerity of your interest, just so both sides can feel more confident about the agreement they are entering into for what will hopefully be a long-term collaboration.

So I have my written offer—how do I conduct a PNC?

First and foremost, ask yourself if this is an offer you would actually accept. If not, save yourself and them the trouble and respectfully decline (we'll cover how to do this later in this chapter). However, if you are genuinely considering this opportunity, a PNC is totally appropriate.

As mentioned earlier, you'd email whoever made you the offer to set up a future call. This time it will be to ask some questions about the offer rather than about the time you have to decide, and during this call you would take them through the offer, line by line, asking, "Do you have any flexibility around [salary]?," "Do you have any flexibility around [signing bonus]?," "Do you have any flexibility around [vacation time]?," and so on. Relocation, unpaid time off, paid sick leave, stock options, housing stipends, annual bonus, and everything else you can think of should be included in the list of questions you should ask.

They won't actually answer "yes" to these, will they?

Not usually. However, there is a huge difference between hearing a flat "no" versus a hem-and-haw "Well, we don't have much wiggle room on that . . ." The latter means "yes," but your contact from human resources would get fired if they gave you a straight yes, just as they'd get fired if they made a habit of giving prospective employees the maximum possible offer in their initial offer letter.

So make a note of where you receive a flat "no" (which means no) versus a more ambiguous answer (which means yes). And if you get an actual "yes," consider that a screaming green light to negotiate on that particular item!

What if they ask me how much of a salary increase or days of vacation I want?

Do *not* negotiate in this phone call. State that you are just trying to fully understand the offer so your next call with them can be as productive for both sides as possible.

By the end of the call, you will have indications of which items in the offer have room for negotiation and which do not. This allows for your *actual* negotiation call to be as smooth as possible, since you'll know to focus only (or mostly) on those items that seemed to be in play with room for movement. This call will take place one or more days after your PNC.

So how does the actual negotiation call go?

I am a firm adherent to the principles-based negotiation strategy presented in Fisher, Ury, and Patton's seminal book on this topic, *Getting to Yes*. While they don't recommend a PNC (which I absolutely do), they help remove the awkwardness and stigma around negotiation to get you to see the other person as a partner rather than an adversary in your negotiation through four basic tenets:

1. Separate the people from the problem (this isn't personal).
2. Focus on interests rather than positions (this is most relevant to us for this chapter).
3. Generate a variety of options before settling on an agreement.
4. Insist that the agreement will be based on objective criteria (this one, too, will prove relevant).[1]

The company wants to bring in a great candidate and focus on other things besides filling empty positions, and you want the best package you can get; these interests are not necessarily at odds with one another!

So how do I conduct a principles-based negotiation?

I can't possibly do *Getting to Yes* justice in the space we have here—in a single negotiation it can potentially make you hundreds (or thousands) of dollars per hour for just that handful of hours it takes you to read it, and you'd enjoy its benefits for the rest of your life—but for our abridged purposes, you will invite your negotiation partner to help you address your interests ("I'm hoping to make a down payment on a condo, since I'm hoping to make a long-term commitment to your company and this area") rather than your positions ("I will accept nothing less than $70,000!").

In short, this means you need to have a "because" for every request you make.

What does having a "because" mean?

Your "because" is a rationale you can share for *why* what you are asking for makes sense. This helps you avoid positional bargaining (like insisting on a particular salary figure without context or rationale, which tends to just make both sides dig in their heels).

But don't I just want as much as I can get?

Of course. The funny thing about having a "because" is that *it doesn't even have to make perfect sense*. Research shows that the mere existence of a "because" is enough to dramatically improve your odds of success. To illustrate, let me introduce you to the copy machine study.

In the 1970s, Ellen Langer and her research team conducted an experiment in which they attempted to cut in line to use a Xerox photocopier in a busy office environment. They found that the success of the request was 60 percent in the control case, where the experimenter simply said, "Excuse me, I have five pages. May I use the Xerox machine?" Not bad.

They found that the success rate jumped to 94 percent when there was a reason for the request, as in "Excuse me, I have five pages. May I use the Xerox machine, because I'm in a rush?" So, that tells us that if you have a great reason, use it! Your success rate jumps by over half!

However, their third finding (Rule of Three alert!) was most interesting. They found that when the experimenter cited a *placebo* (or empty) reason, as in "Excuse me, I have five pages. May I use the Xerox machine, because I need to make copies?," the success rate barely changed, dropping just slightly, to 93 percent.[2]

In other words, it really is the thought that counts; the word "because" is itself an act of deference that makes people more open to whatever it is you are proposing. In negotiation terms, the "because" is a show of good faith that you're not engaging in arbitrary positional bargaining; there are real reasons underlying your request for more, and it's a signal to the employer that you would like the same—for them to provide the reasons why, if they choose to decline your request.

So how do I prepare for a negotiation?

Researching before your actual negotiation is tricky, simply because even if you had perfect information about what the person before you made in that role, the employer has no obligation to offer you the same salary.

Thus, you shouldn't stress yourself out too much looking for accurate information, since it's very easy for the employer to give you a reason why that figure was appropriate for *that* candidate but not appropriate for you. (Alternatively, assume your predecessor's salary was precisely one million dollars. It won't effectively change how you should handle your negotiation once you get *your* actual offer.)

However, information (precise or otherwise) is still helpful. Instead of obsessing over a specific number, however, focus on finding data points that directionally move you in a higher direction. These include average salaries of graduates of your most recent academic program from your alma mater and salary information from employment websites like Glassdoor and PayScale.

Also, if you're relocating for a new role, look up a cost-of-living calculator online. If data shows the cost of living will be 10 percent higher where your new job will be, that's an easy way for you to ask for a bump in salary, as in "I noted that the cost of living is 10 percent higher where you are located. Can you increase the salary at all to help me close that gap?" (Granted, they may have based their offer on *their* location's cost of living, but remember that the specific "because" is less important than *having* a "because" to show that this is a collaborative rather than competitive exercise.)

Next, bring out your list of items from your PNC where it seemed like there could be movement, and come up with a "because" for each one. You may not need to refer to the "because," but it's nice to have one. Some of my favorites are:

- "Can you increase the salary at all? *Because* I have a budget and am trying to pay off my student loans within X years, and that would help me do so."

- "Can you increase the signing bonus at all? *Because* I'm hoping to make a down payment on a house/condo to start putting down roots in this area."

- "Can you provide/increase a relocation stipend at all? *Because* I have loan payments to manage before my start date, and that would help me manage the interim period from a working capital perspective."
- "Can you provide/increase paid vacation time at all? *Because* I have a number of weddings/family events to attend in the coming year."
- "Can you increase the stock options piece of the compensation at all? *Because* I'd like for my success to match the company's overall success."

   . . . and so on.

Again, what if they say no?

Feel free to ask why not. You have given them some logic by providing your "because" and, wherever possible, offering data that supports your request; hopefully they will do the same, and in doing so impart some clues about where some flexibility in the offer may be available, as in "We can't move on salary at all, because your start class is all making the same amount in your first year. We may be able to move a bit on relocation or signing bonus, but that's about it." Aha! Relocation and signing bonus it is, and no hard feelings!

You will find that employers care more about certain buckets of money (like salary) more than others (one-time payments like a relocation and signing bonus or noncash items like vacation or flexible work arrangements). These won't often be volunteered at the outset, but if you open a negotiation, many hiring managers (in their own self-interest, trying to help you max out your compensation while maximizing the odds that they can end this search process ASAP) may try to steer you the right way.

Just be ready to be creative. This will be more of a collaborative dance than a debate, so keeping an open mind about what an acceptable solution looks like may help you find it.

So what topic should I negotiate on first?

I would open the discussion with salary, since that will be most important to both sides. If you are going to get a hard "no" on anything, it will be salary, so if you sense salary is a dead end, you can pivot to other options where they will feel increasing desire to give you some sort of a win for putting forth a respectful effort.

In any case, you should always negotiate. For a more thorough discussion about the art of negotiation, I encourage you to read *Getting to Yes* by Roger Fisher.

OK, so it feels like the employer has moved as much as they are going to move on this offer. Should I accept on the spot?

I recommend not doing so.

In general, I advise always taking at least a night between the negotiation and the acceptance or decline. Let the adrenaline from your negotiation leave your system so you can make the most clearheaded decision possible. Ideally, I recommend making sure you have two nights to make the decision.

Two nights is just enough time for you to try my favorite technique for this situation: the Sleep on It exercise—my pet (and fan-favorite) approach for holistically deciding whether to accept an offer, or whether to accept one offer versus another.

How does the Sleep on It exercise work?

It's simple. It consists only of doing a brain dump of all the pros and cons of accepting an offer so they are out of your head and into a list. Add to this list throughout the day as more pros and cons come to mind. This isn't about seeing whether accepting the offer has more pros rather than cons; it's more about offloading them, ensuring that you do not constantly cycle through them one at a time in your head all day or, equally bad, forget one or more of them.

Then, as you are preparing for bed, imagine you have accepted the offer.

Like, *really* imagine it. Don't fixate, but just begin your night's rest carrying yourself as the person who just accepted that offer. Then drift off to sleep . . . with a pen and paper on your nightstand.

When you wake, write down how you feel about having (pretend) accepted the offer. Elated at working with your new colleagues? Relieved that your search is over? Nauseous at having cut off other opportunities?

The next night, reverse the exercise: imagine you've *declined* the offer (or accepted a different one, if you received multiple offers), repeat the steps, and see how you feel the *following* morning.

I find that the body is surprisingly wonderful at holistically simulating and processing regret, yet it is woefully ineffective at holistically simulating and processing happiness. Too many job seekers focus on the elusiveness of the latter instead of embracing the instructiveness of the former. Let the body do what it does best, which is repairing itself overnight to prepare us for the following day. Did you just make your body's job easier by accepting that offer, or harder?

Like it or not, the job search is *not* a purely rational exercise, no matter how hard I try to make its interim steps feel that way. In the end, the heart wants what it wants; the body just follows the heart's lead.

Similarly, I don't know exactly why this exercise's focus on avoiding regret proves so clarifying for job seekers; I just know that it does. In fact, I've had former students contact me out of the blue years later to thank me for sharing that exercise with them years earlier. It's simple, easy, and immediate. (Just ensure you allow yourself a couple of consecutive nights to conduct the exercise.)

What if my body prefers a course of action that isn't reasonable?

If it were truly unreasonable, I'd argue it wasn't a real option in the first place!

However, if it just seems unlikely rather than unreasonable, ask yourself what about it is making your body such a big fan? Is there a way you can split that difference? Talk it over with your close friends and loved ones and explain your conflict to them; they may help you see perspectives, options, or resources for more information that you can't see on your own.

That said, I'd rather you be excited to get to work when you wake up every morning—even if there is an acceptable measure of risk involved—rather than postponing happiness for months, years, or longer without even trying. Regret is a slow-acting poison. You can't outrun it or ignore it; it will exact its toll on you eventually. If life circumstances, such as financial responsibilities, force you to take a role you will regret, recognize that you won't be able to keep that position forever before your own health suffers, potentially depleting your ability to fulfill your financial responsibilities at all. Therefore, start planning and enacting your pivot immediately, as it could take weeks, months, or even years, depending on your ability to devote time to it. (If you have not already read it, *2HJS* will help you create this plan and put it into action as painlessly and effectively as possible.)

However, even a setback in terms of salary, status, or stability—if it results in you rediscovering a hunger to be better that you may have lost—will be short term if you are improving at your craft every day, whereas standing pat would result in continued stagnation that only becomes more taxing with age.

The Sleep on It Exercise isn't the be-all, end-all of decision-making when it comes to offer selection, but I find that it is very enlightening in a way that counting pros and cons or acting out of fear are not. Give your body a chance to weigh in, and you will be impressed with how much sense it makes.

OK, I performed the Sleep on It Exercise, and I'm in! How do I accept?

Feel free to do so over email, phone, or video—whichever you prefer. Sometimes getting them the decision ASAP is more helpful to them than setting up another future call, so use your best judgment.

However, your work is not done! Once you accept an offer, you *must* inform your network that you are off the market. The quickest way to lose an advocate at a different company is to let them fight for you, unaware, after you've ceased being available; they will have spent political capital on your behalf with only embarrassment to show for it.

So send a quick thank-you note to anyone else who may be advocating for you—both at the firm whose offer you are accepting and with other firms you were in conversations with—to express appreciation for their insights that directly or indirectly led you to the good news you have finally achieved. This will prevent their fruitlessly advocating on your behalf and preserve their advocacy for any future searches.

That being said, the far more important topic is making sure you know how to decline an offer.

Don't worry—it's easier than you think.

So how do I decline an offer?

I recommend treating this much as you would a request to extend your offer deadline. Email them, explain that you have a time-sensitive update regarding your status, and ask if they can connect by phone at their earliest possible convenience (again, don't do this over a weekend).

The phone or video chat may be very short: you thank them for the offer and explain to them that you have decided to decline, giving them a little of the rationale that led you to do so.

Can't I just email them my offer decline?

You could, but it may be considered bad form, given the hours that person and/or organization has spent getting to know you.

That said, if they ask you what you would like to chat about rather than set up a call with you straightaway, I'd say you are free to share your decline over email, and—since it is safe to say that email will be widely forwarded around the organization to spread the word—immediately notify your strongest advocates of your decision so they don't have to find out your decision from a colleague's forwarded email; at least they will have received a personalized message from you thanking them for their time.

In any case, I recommend having an irreconcilable difference ready when declining an offer, should anyone ask you why you are declining (which they will).

What's an irreconcilable difference?

It's a reason this employer can't readily match, like another offer for work in a different part of the country, the chance to work in a different sector than the ones in which that employer operates, a much larger or smaller company or team size—you get the idea.

I have seen job seekers say the opportunity to work at home is their reason for taking a different company's offer, only to learn that the employer they are declining *also* allowed employees to work from home. Pretty awkward! Try to find something the employer you are declining can't (or won't or didn't when given the chance) match.

Finally, once you've accepted an offer and notified the rest of your network that you are now off the market, be sure to celebrate the end of (this iteration of) your job search journey!

CHAPTER CHECKLIST	
Do you know to email thank-you notes after every interview?	✓
Do you know how to request an offer extension (*not* over email) if you need more time to decide?	✓
Do you know how to set up and conduct a PNC to probe for flexibility in the offer prior to the negotiation itself?	✓
Have you created a "because" for every offer negotiation item you plan to request?	✓
Have you found a copy of *Getting to Yes* to read? (Seriously. Just read it.)	✓
Do you know how to complete the Sleep on It Exercise to determine whether or not to accept a particular offer?	✓
Do you know to notify advocates at other firms once you've accepted an offer?	✓
Do you know how to decline an offer?	✓

TROUBLESHOOTING

What if the offer is better than I was expecting? Should I still try to negotiate?

Yes! Remember, respectfully attempting to negotiate makes your new employer feel better about the hire they're about to make, since they can't trust those who won't even negotiate for themselves to negotiate on behalf of the company. (They may also question whether they overpaid you given your instant acceptance!)

Plus, again, it's very unlikely they made you their absolute best offer in their initial offer letter. Most employers hold at least something back so that they can give you something to reward you for negotiating.

What if the offer they make me is *much lower* than expected?

If it's in the same ballpark, it's likely they are just leaving *lots* of room for negotiation.

However, if it's insultingly low (compared to market rates, not compared to the million dollars I told you to assume earlier in this chapter!), it's worth having a frank conversation (again, *not* in an email) with whoever made you the offer to ask why the offer was so far out of line with expectations (it could be that it is heavily weighted toward equity or annual bonuses for high performers rather than fixed salary) to see if the gap can be bridged at all, instead of entering into a more traditional negotiation.

Employers don't want to waste time interviewing candidates they can't afford, so hopefully employers who suspect you are out of their price range will raise this issue sooner rather than later, but from time to time one does not, in the hopes that you will be desperate and/or mentally invested by that point that they might get you at a heavy discount.

CHAPTER 9

Coffee Chats and Weekly Manager Meetings

Won't my new job consist of more than just coffee chats and weekly manager meetings?

Yes. Tons more. Like, nearly your entire new job will be things *other* than coffee chats and weekly manager meetings.

However, whenever I talk to job seekers who either don't get return offers at the end of an internship or don't get promoted on time, it is almost always due to a lack of internal advocacy on their behalf within the organization. These two techniques—coffee chats and weekly manager meetings—are two simple, reliable tools that help ensure that you, too, will not suffer from a lack of internal advocacy within your organization after you start.

However, despite the power of coffee chats and weekly manager meetings to help keep your path to full-time employment and/or advancement on track, they are both widely underutilized and woefully underdiscussed. If either is mentioned at all, they are glossed over with some general tips.

But you should know by now that I don't do tips. I do instructions.

Thus we are going to discuss each of these techniques in depth. Coffee chats are informational meetings that you'd conduct once you're on board at a new employer. I recommend using the TIARA Framework that I mentioned in chapters 1 and 7 (and which I covered in depth in *The 2-Hour Job Search*) for the conversations themselves; this chapter will instead cover how to *deploy* TIARA-based coffee chats at a strategic level to maximize your chance of return offers and/or advancement at promotion time.

What do you mean "deploy" coffee chats?

Like revenge (but unlike coffee itself), coffee chats are a technique best served cold, meaning they should be conducted *after* the initial wave of introductory meetings you conduct with your new teammates.

(If you have no such introductory meetings set up for you by your new employer, I recommend setting them up with any person you are likely to be interacting with regularly in order to complete your projects; you should feel free to make these as social or as work-related as your contact prefers.)

If you are at a larger organization or part of a "start class" (a number of people starting the same position at the same organization at approximately the same time), these initial rounds of introductory meetings will often be scheduled for you and would be points of parity rather than points of differentiation, as we discussed in chapter 4; they will not put you at an advantage over the other members of your start class or organization, since they show no initiative on your part—you merely showed up where you were told to.

Coffee chats, on the other hand, differ from introductory meetings in timing, audience, or both, and their focus at least initially tends to be more on learning (which tends to lead to advocacy) than on functional rapport-building.

How do coffee chats differ in timing from introductory meetings?

Coffee chats tend to occur several weeks after your introductory meetings. This allows you to get a basic understanding of your role and be better able to hold an informed conversation (which tends to result from

TIARA Framework–structured meetings) about the work that your colleagues do: the Trends they are facing, the Insights they've had over the years, and so on.

That's tougher to do right after you start, when you are still orienting to your new role and organization, and you risk short-circuiting rapport if you try to cram all of TIARA into an introductory get-to-know-you meeting!

Makes sense, but how do coffee chats differ in audience from introductory meetings?

You'd conduct coffee chats with those you've had introductory meetings with (now that you've seen them in action a bit more and grasp what their role on your team is, what challenges they face, and so on) *as well as* with a broader audience of people whose work interests you, whether or not you'd be directly interacting with them.

Why is it helpful to network with people outside my work team?

Nobody tells you this, but when so-called "calibration meetings" happen at your organization—essentially, when an organization ranks employees at a particular level by calling all their managers into the room to decide whom to retain and whom to advance—you are *expected* to get support from your manager. Again, it's a point of parity rather than a point of differentiation.

And you can't even always guarantee that your manager is going to fight for you, even if you have a good working relationship. Some managers aren't the type to speak up vigorously for their reports in these meetings, even when their reports are solid performers. Other managers could be thinking of leaving the organization themselves and have already mentally checked out, and so on. Or your manager could be sick that day.

In other words, when it comes to internal advocacy, you can't rely *solely* on your manager—or your immediate work team, who won't usually be in the room for calibration meetings. You need to broaden your advocacy base, and that means setting up coffee chats with people who otherwise wouldn't get to see you in action. This *especially* means "reaching out sideways."

What is "reaching out sideways"?

It is the act of setting up coffee chats with managers at your immediate supervisor's level but with whom you don't directly work. Reaching out sideways is the *single* best technique for maximizing the impact of the coffee chats you conduct, since those managers will often be involved in calibration meetings.

To be clear, you should mention to your supervisor that you will be reaching out sideways, conducting meetings similar to the ones you've already conducted with them, so they won't think you are going behind their back.

(As an aside, here's one other suggestion: if you are part of a start class at a larger organization, ask around among your peers to see who likes their manager a lot, and set up coffee chats with *those* managers in particular. If you don't know your start class peers well enough to ask this question, set up coffee chat "friend dates" with some of them as well! Well-liked managers tend to be disproportionately influential during calibration meetings, given their broad social capital, so having a relationship with them is invaluable—it may also lay the groundwork for your working for them in the future, and no single factor improves your odds at promotion more than having a great manager.)

That said, don't limit yourself to *just* people at your manager's level, lest your networking efforts seem too on the nose. Really, just set them up with anyone you cross paths with whom you seem to have rapport with, regardless of their area, and those whom you see doing interesting work within your organization. You don't need a permit for this! Just let your immediate manager know that you find value in learning from others within the organization, and once you have their blessing to do so, you can invite whomever you want to meet up.

How do I set up a coffee chat?

Simply email the person you'd like to have a coffee chat with and ask them if they could spare some time in the coming week or two to share their insights with you over coffee.

Put in more effort than that and you risk either talking about yourself too much (remember that these conversations are more about them than you, so your email should reflect that selfless ethos) or transparently flattering your contact. Neither is desirable or necessary. Keep it casual but respectful, with just a hint of deference.

How long are these meetings?

Usually about thirty minutes. Very busy executives may limit your conversation to fifteen minutes, and others may offer forty-five minutes or lunch. Accept whatever time your contact offers.

What if I (or they) don't like coffee?

Feel free to swap in tea, water, a walk, or simply enjoying some sunshine together outside in an atrium or (if remote) on your respective porches. The coffee is merely an excuse to get together.

If in person, should I pay for the coffee?

Typically, the person who requests the meeting would treat for coffee, but you'll find you will often be overruled if you attempt to pay for a superior's drink, and that is totally fine. (They may even have an expense account for such meetings.) Either way, don't force it. Norms will differ from person to person, organization to organization, and sector to sector.

My preferred approach is to ask "May I treat?" in my first meeting or two within an organization, and gauge from their reaction whether that is a welcome gesture and whether that is comfortable for you. (And affordable! Don't feel obligated to treat if the only coffee available is $12 single-source shade-grown artisanal coffee. Hopefully your organization pays people at the manager level enough to cover their own coffee, in that case!)

What's the potential outcome of a coffee chat?

In the TIARA Framework, you'll make a habit of asking what Advice your contacts have for you and what Resources they recommend you look into next, so take careful notes during this part of the conversation (yes, you'll be taking notes during the chat; failing to do so may imply that you don't find what they're sharing with you to be particularly interesting).

You'll send a thank-you note within a day or so after your coffee chat, and you'll set a reminder for a few weeks from now. When that reminder pops up, that is your signal to check back in with the potential internal advocate to thank them again and *report back the results* of following the Advice they gave you or looking into the Resources they recommended. Nothing makes a mentor feel better than being told that the advice they had already forgotten giving made a material impact on a (now) mentee.

Do this, and more often than not you'll have created an advocate for life within that organization, and quite possibly beyond as well— helping you secure that full-time offer, next promotion, or even different job opportunities at the advocate's future organizations as well!

OK, coffee chats—check. What about weekly manager meetings? Are they what I think they are?

You mean meetings you have with your manager each week? Yes, but they are *sooo* much more than that, when used well.

Many novice professionals treat these as free-form conversations, but I *strongly* recommend using this time in a much more purposeful, thoughtful manner. Freestyling these conversations leaves too much to chance about how well your manager will appreciate your effort, value your output, and advocate for you at review time.

A simple one-page document that you produce to review (and leave) with your manager helps ensure that they (1) know what you've accomplished in the past week, (2) understand your priorities for the coming week (so they can change them around, if desired), and (3) can observe that you are proactively working to improve.

If you've done all those three things, your success (or lack thereof) becomes more of a reflection on your supervisor than you, so they are highly incentivized to go to bat for you at promotion time.

How do I get a weekly manager meeting?

Just ask.

Especially when you're starting out, you have the license to ask a lot of questions and request regular check-ins to ensure you are working on the right things in the right way. Weekly updates with your manager could be offered to you as you get up to speed (and then they may taper to every other week once you get more established). If they are not, though, it is worth explicitly requesting for all parties' benefit.

What if my manager says they don't have time for a weekly meeting?

This is concerning. I imagine this response is most likely if you are a temporary intern. If that is the case, it's even *more* important that they are regularly apprised of your work, given your limited time frame in which to show results.

Ask them (over coffee, ideally—*not* over email!) if the issue is the duration of the meeting—if so, these can be condensed to fifteen-minute meetings if necessary. If it is something else, ask for more information so you can understand how best to keep your manager updated on your work and possibly identify items you can take off their plate to make their life easier (the hallmark of any excellent direct report).

At the end of the day, your work is your manager's work, so it's critical that you get aligned. Even five dedicated minutes every week to make sure you don't head off in the wrong direction work-wise is better than an hour every month, which inevitably leads to disaster, in terms of both satisfaction and progress.

So what gets covered in weekly manager meetings?

It's really simple. Here are the items I recommend covering in an ideal Weekly Manager Meeting (WMM) agenda (going forward, I will use the capitalized version to describe a meeting that uses the following format, and the lowercase generic term "weekly manager meeting" otherwise).

1. Updates (from the previous week)
2. Priorities (for the coming week, in order of importance)
3. Additional Priorities (as time permits)
4. Questions

(Note: A downloadable template for your WMM agenda is available at 2hourjobsearch.com/resources.)

Why start with updates from the previous week?

A common issue many new employees face at evaluation time—either their annual review or even earlier during their thirty-, sixty-, or ninety-day trial period before they become full-fledged employees—is that they don't have accomplishments to point to. The Updates section of your WMM agenda ensures that you don't fall into this trap: just suddenly making one of your priorities disappear because it has been completed doesn't have the same lasting impact as an update highlighting its on-time completion and any remarkable results.

Come evaluation time, your work is only as good as your manager's ability to explain it, so here is the chance to highlight for your supervisor when a priority has been accomplished, what complications you ran into, and what insights you had that led to any above-average results.

Isn't this self-promotion awkward?

Yes, but you need to view this self-promotion as a service you are providing to your supervisor. They will often be asked by *their* supervisors how you are doing, so giving them a soundbite to share with their higher-ups makes them look good as well, creating a win-win.

Why do I need to share my priorities for the week? My supervisor sets my priorities!

It ensures that your supervisor is aware of your workload, that you have captured *all* of your priorities and—even more importantly—that you are attacking them in the right order.

Under the Priorities section of your agenda, list your priorities in order of importance to ensure that you both agree on their relative importance and/or the order in which they should be tackled. Often, one or more of them will feature a bottleneck—a waiting period following a request for information, resources, or assistance that will not necessarily be immediately available. Your supervisor can be incredibly helpful in either pointing out an impending bottleneck or even expediting your navigation of that bottleneck now that you've reminded them you will need that handled in order to get your work done. (Remember, they have their own priorities, so these meetings are often the only time you can ensure that they fully empathize with the priorities you have on your plate.)

What if I don't have time to complete all of my priorities for the week?!

The agenda you've prepared makes that conversation much easier to have. You can show your supervisor what you plan to tackle in which order, and estimate for them what you can complete in the coming week.

Items that you will not be able to get to this week would be moved to the Additional Priorities section for future efforts beyond that week.

What if my manager also needs that additional priority done this week?

The agenda allows you to discuss your workload with your manager to ensure that it is sustainable. (Note that the definition of "sustainable" will vary widely by industry; "sustainable" to an investment banker would be a labor violation for most of the rest of us, but we all make choices!)

If your manager wants a particular item completed this week, the WMM agenda allows you to reach agreement with your manager about which of your current active priorities can and should be deprioritized (that is, moved down to the Additional Priorities section) to make room for the more time-sensitive item.

What if it is our busy season and everything needs to get done?

Sometimes everything just simply needs to get done, whether it's to hit a major deadline or to correct an error. In that case, you either bite the bullet and work overtime or, if that is simply not possible, communicate with your teammates and your supervisor. If a short-term disruption compromises your ability to get your work done, schedule an in-person meeting with your teammates to see if you can work out an arrangement where they cover for you until you are able to take back the full share of your work. If a long-term disruption arises or if your teammates are unable to assist with the short-term tasks, meet with your manager to see if any accommodations can be made to help you get your work done in a different fashion—by working remotely, for example, or working a modified work day/week.

This WMM conversation allows you to confirm that this is indeed busy season (or if *every* week is busy season, meaning you need to address the unsustainable status quo before your manager interprets your silence as tacit agreement) as well as gain permission to bill that overtime (where applicable) and/or arrange for personal time in the future to account for your overage this particular week.

Norms vary by employer and sector, but you don't want to bill overtime if your employer has a strict policy against it, nor do you want to be logging "busy season" hours outside of busy season, since that is simply not sustainable, nor is that the job you signed up for.

However, I *strongly* discourage "going along to get along" when starting a new job. It is much harder to change your work pattern to be more sustainable a few months in than it is to establish effective boundaries up front. That doesn't mean drawing a hard line in the sand; it just means openly communicating with your supervisor when you are working at an unsustainable rate that does not match the expectations they set for you when you accepted that role. This ensures that this situation is indeed temporary and helps identify measures that can be taken to improve your quality of life in the interim, be it approval to order in meals to the office or leeway to take a half-day the following week to run errands.

What is the Questions section of the WMM agenda for?

This was an innovation by my own direct report at Duke, David Solloway. He's a master listener. (Truly, it's inspiring.) He also personifies lifelong learning, and he created this section of the WMM to pick my brain about both questions he had that helped him accomplish his priorities and also questions about more general knowledge: higher education, career services, coaching, writing, professional speaking, and a variety of other topics (he usually had one or two a week, with more being more common during slower times of year).

I'd like to say I taught him a lot during these meetings with my responses to his questions, but I don't know that for sure; only Dave can say for certain. But as his boss, that's kind of a weird question for me to ask him, so I'm just going to assume I was awesome.

What I do know for certain is how much I *liked* being asked these questions! Nobody else ever asked me about where I thought our industry was headed in five years, how I manage a tricky stakeholder relationship, how I balance work with writing, and so on and so forth!

Not only did I enjoy how smart they made me feel (and how they forced me to clarify and codify my own thinking about my work in an understandable, accessible way), but they also demonstrated to me that Dave was genuinely engaging in his role and striving to take his work to the next level.

So while I can't say for sure that Dave benefited from getting his questions answered, I know that I, as his boss, definitely benefited from answering them. It's a fun way to end your WMM, always ending on a learning note that allows your supervisor to show off some of their hard-fought wisdom. Who wouldn't like that?

So I leave this WMM agenda with my supervisor?

Yes, email in advance and/or print out two hard copies of your WMM agenda (if company policy allows) so you may make notes on one and leave the other with your supervisor to file away as they wish.

For me as a manager, my folder of past agendas of my own direct reports (including Dave) is invaluable at jogging my own memory about historical projects we had discussed, major accomplishments my report has achieved during this fiscal year, and how quickly certain projects have progressed or are progressing. All are useful, and those WMM summaries are much easier to flip through to grasp the highlights of my report's work than a bunch of email folders.

And that's it! Again, there is so much more to your job than just coffee chats and weekly manager meetings, but when a new hire flames out in the new role, it tends to be due to lack of advocacy rather than lack of talent, work ethic, or insight.

Coffee chats and structured WMMs help minimize the risk that you will lack sufficient advocacy at review time to reach that next level, on or ahead of schedule!

CHAPTER CHECKLIST	
Do you know when, with whom, and how to request, conduct, and follow up on coffee chats?	✓
Do you understand the importance of "reaching out sideways"?	✓
Do you know the benefits of conducting structured WMMs?	✓
Do you know how to conduct a structured WMM?	✓

TROUBLESHOOTING

What if a contact doesn't respond to my coffee chat request?

I recommend following up once and only once. When you send your invite, set a reminder in your calendar for a week later and then forget about this person until they either respond or your reminder pops up, signaling it's time for you to follow up with them.

For that follow-up, I would forward the previous message and above it add language like this: "Hi Avery, I just wanted to follow up to see if now is a better time to connect. Might you have some time to meet up for coffee in the coming week or two?"

If they ignore your follow-up message, they are not interested. Feel free to move on to other contacts at that point, if you haven't already!

What if my manager cancels our WMM?

Attempt to reschedule, especially if you are on an internship or short-term contract. You don't have that much time to accomplish what you need to, so losing a couple of weeks due to having your priorities in the wrong order or not addressing a bottleneck early enough could be devastating.

Now, if your manager goes on vacation and doesn't offer to connect during that time, you may be out of luck, but see if you can at least ensure alignment over email during short-term work engagements (or at least get your manager to designate a proxy manager for you to report to in their absence). If not, ask the other mentors you've developed in that organization what they'd do in your position, so at least you know one person will approve of the executive decisions you may be required to make in your manager's absence, come evaluation time!

If these cancellations become chronic, it's fair to discuss this with your manager to better understand whether they feel the meetings are too frequent or not helpful to them, to see if you can find an arrangement and timing that helps you get your job done but also is respectful of their time.

Dave and I met weekly for our first couple of years, but after he gained more experience, we were able to switch to once every two weeks, with brief check-ins during the interim as necessary. We simply didn't need to connect as often to review his work as we did when he was just starting out.

Either way, whenever possible, if you sense your manager is not communicating something to you explicitly, feel free to ask about it. It may grant you peace of mind that nothing is going on, or it may allow for a more honest exchange of ideas and concerns that allow both of you to do your jobs better and more comfortably.

CONCLUSION

"The job search is an art, not a science" has always seemed like a massive cop-out to me. Art is beautiful and unique, but employers are generally seeking pretty standard things when they read your cover letter or ask you, "Why do you want to work for our company?"

So, in response to "It's an art, not a science," I respectfully say, *"Really?"*

Some of the approaches in the book may have surprised you. Some may have upset you. Some may have caused you to question the nature of life itself. (In that last case, please do go see someone. That is an extreme reaction to a job search book.) I wanted to challenge your thinking on these subjects that for far too long have been called art, despite their relative uniformity, which I hope is now apparent.

Personally, I think there is art in practicing science well. Great bakers can do amazing things within the constraints of a particular recipe, and that is what I hope for each and every one of you. Start with these recipes to get a foothold quickly in each phase of your job search, and then find your own artistic expression within rather than starting from scratch.

And as with *2HJS*, I don't expect that all sections will move everyone equally. It was set up like a cookbook for that reason; you can simply review the recipes and find the ones that work best for you and quickly forget about the rest.

However, I want to thank you for even considering these recipes.

I hope you found what you were looking for in the preceding pages. At the very least, I hope you feel less anxiety about your job search now, having discovered some new approaches that make your job search easier and simpler, not harder and more complicated.

Perhaps it will lead you to come up with your own recipes. If so, please do share with me what you came up with! The world truly is a better place when we can all sample each other's home cooking.

ACKNOWLEDGMENTS

I'm humbled that I even get to do this, so let me briefly thank the people who helped bring these recipes to fruition.

- My family—I truly couldn't have done this without your support.

- My Fuqua Programs Team partners-in-crime, David Solloway and Shawn Pulscher—this book simply wouldn't exist without the two of you, as your fingerprints are all over these concepts, from RAC to How Your Talents Add Value to WMMs and beyond. Your work inspires me daily, and I consider myself lucky to be your colleague.

- Rebecca Gonzales—you've been my beloved ride-or-die throughout this process. Thank you for your patience, support, understanding, (capital R) Responsibility, and steady stream of delicious baked goods.

- My agent, Richard Morris—thank you for your years of steady insight and confidence in my books' potential.

- My editors, Kimmy Tejasindhu and Julie Bennett at Ten Speed Press— just because it's my second book doesn't mean I'm a better writer this time! Thank you for making this content suitable for all audiences.

- Peter DiCola, Nadeem Hussain, Tim Nangle, Jean Ro, Javier Izquierdo, Brett Lasher, Amanda Ray, and Melissa Gudell—for everything.

- My amazing Career Management Center colleagues at Fuqua, past and present. Your insights have also lifted every concept in this text, and your enduring support has meant the world to me.

- All of my Facebook brainstormers—all those analogy requests really did have a purpose!

- And you for giving this book a chance.

ABOUT THE AUTHOR

STEVE DALTON is the author of *The 2 Hour Job Search*, founder and CEO of the corporate training firm Contact2Colleague, and a senior career consultant and program director at Duke University's Fuqua School of Business. He holds an MBA from the same institution. Prior to entering the career services industry, Steve was a twice-promoted strategy consultant with A. T. Kearney and an associate marketing manager at General Mills. He lives in Durham, North Carolina. Visit www.2hourjobsearch.com and www.contact2colleague.com for inquiries, follow Steve on Twitter at @Dalton_Steve, and join his books' LinkedIn Group at "The 2-Hour Job Search—Q&A Forum."

NOTES

Chapter 1

1. Camilo Maldonado, "Price of College Increasing Almost 8 Times Faster Than Wages," *Forbes*, July 24, 2018, https://www.forbes.com/sites /camilomaldonado/2018/07/24/price-of-college-increasing-almost-8-times-faster-than-wages/#d00905c66c1d.

2. Federal Reserve Bank of St. Louis, "Real Median Household Income in the United States," *FRED Newsletter*, September 10, 2019, https://fred.stlouisfed.org/series/MEHOINUSA672N.

3. Institute of Education Sciences, National Center for Education Statistics, "The National Postsecondary Student Aid Study (NPSAS)" (n.d.), https://nces.ed.gov/fastfacts/display.asp?id=76.

4. Drew DeSilver, "For Most U.S. Workers, Real Wages Have Barely Budged in Decades," Pew Research Center FACTTANK, August 7, 2018, https://www.pewresearch.org/fact-tank/2018/08/07/for-most-us-workers-real-wages-have-barely-budged-for-decades.

5. Meta Brown, Elizabeth Setren, and Giorgio Topa, "Do Informal Referrals Lead to Better Matches? Evidence from a Firm's Employee Referral System," *Journal of Labor Economics* 34, no. 1 (January 2016): 161–209.

Chapter 2

1. Susan Adams, "What Your Resume Is Up Against," *Forbes*, March 26, 2012, https://www.forbes.com/sites/susanadams/2012/03/26 /what-your-resume-is-up-against/#62b76fdf3f9c.

2. Horst Siebert, *Der Kobra-Effekt: Wie Man Irrwege der Wirtschaftspolitik Vermeidet* (in German) (Munich: Deutsche Verlags-Anstalt, 2001).

3. Dona Collins, "The 500-Year Evolution of the Resume," *Business Insider*, February 12, 2011, https://www.businessinsider.com /how-resumes-have-evolved-since-their-first-creation-in-1482-2011-2#resumes-become-an-institution-2.

Chapter 5

1. Rachel E. Frieder, Chad H. Van Iddekinge, and Patrick H. Raymark, "How Quickly Do Interviewers Reach Decisions? An Examination of Interviewers' Decision-Making Time Across Applicants," *Journal of Occupational and Organizational Psychology* 89, no. 2 (June 2016): 223–248.

2. Gordon H. Bower and Michal C. Clark, "Narrative Stories as Mediators for Serial Learning," *Psychonomic Science* 14, no. 4 (April 1969): 181–182.

Chapter 7

1. Donald A Redelmeier, Joel Katz, and Daniel Kahneman, "Memories of Colonoscopy: A Randomized Trial," *Pain* 104, nos. 1–2 (2003): 187–194.

2. Robert B. Cialdini, *Influence: The Psychology of Persuasion* (New York: HarperCollins, 1984).

Chapter 8

1. Roger Fisher, William Ury, and Bruce Patton, *Getting to Yes: Negotiating Agreement Without Giving In*, 3rd ed., rev. ed. (New York: Penguin, 2011).

2. Ellen Langer, Arthur Blank, and Benzion Chanowitz, "The Mindlessness of Ostensibly Thoughtful Action: The Role of 'Placebic' Information in Interpersonal Interaction," *Journal of Personality and Social Psychology* 36, no. 6 (1978): 635–642.

INDEX

LinkedIn profiles
About section in, 54
Accomplishments section in, 57
Education section in, 55–56
80/20 rule and, 50–51
Experience section in, 55
headlines in, 52–54
headshots for, 52
Interests section in, 57
interface changes and, 58
Licenses & Certifications section in, 56
Premium membership and, 50
Recommendations section in, 56–57
resumes and, 51–52
Skills & Endorsements section in, 56
Volunteer Experience section in, 56

M

marginalized community members, 140–41
meetings. *See* calibration meetings; coffee chats; informational meetings; introductory meetings; weekly manager meetings

N

negotiation, 148–51, 153–58, 163. *See also* prenegotiation call
networking, 2, 3, 4, 9–10

O

Odyssey Planning, 19
offers
accepting or declining, 148, 152, 158–62
better than expected, 163

lower than expected, 163
negotiating, 148–51, 153–58, 163
prenegotiation calls and, 151–53
rescinded, 151
written, 152

P

PAR (Problem-Action-Result), 108
Pareto principle. *See* 80/20 rule
parity, points of, 65
Parker, Trey, 84
peak-end rule, 134–35
perverse incentives, 34–35
positive psychology, 14
prenegotiation call (PNC), 151–53
Pulscher, Shawn and Maureen, 99

R

RAC (Reason-Anecdote-Connection) Model, 61, 62–68, 96–102
"reaching out sideways," 167
reading mindfully, 18
Ready-to-Eat (RTE) approach, 115–17, 129
Reasons. *See* RAC (Reason-Anecdote-Connection) Model
Research and Rapport (R&R) questions, 138–39
responsibility statements, 40–41
Result. *See* CAR (Challenge-Action-Result) stories
resumes
accomplishment statements in, 40–42, 48–49
Additional Information section in, 46, 79
Basic vs. Good vs. Great, 30–32, 40–42, 47
bullet points in, 27–29, 32–33, 40–42, 44–46, 48–49, 64, 108